PEOPLE
IN THE NEWS

Johnny Depp

by Kara Higgins

**LUCENT
BOOKS®**

THOMSON

™

GALE

San Diego • Detroit • New York • San Francisco • Cleveland
New Haven, Conn. • Waterville, Maine • London • Munich

THOMSON

GALE

On cover: Johnny Depp portrays the romantic outsider Roux in the hit film *Chocolat.*

© 2004 by Lucent Books. Lucent Books is an imprint of The Gale Group, Inc., a division of Thomson Learning, Inc.

Lucent Books® and Thomson Learning™ are trademarks used herein under license.

For more information, contact
Lucent Books
27500 Drake Rd.
Farmington Hills, MI 48331-3535
Or you can visit our Internet site at http://www.gale.com

LIBRARY OF CONGRESS CATALOGING-IN-PUBLICATION DATA

Higgins, Kara.
    Johnny Depp / by Kara Higgins.
        p. cm. — (People in the news)
    ISBN 1-59018-538-2 (lib. bdg. : alk. paper)
    1. Depp, Johnny—Juvenile literature. 2. Motion picture actors and actresses—United States—Biography—Juvenile literature. I. Title. II. Series: People in the news (San Diego, Calif.)
    PN2287.D39H54 2004
    791.4302'8'092—dc22
                                                                    2004000384

Printed in the United States of America

Table of Contents

Foreword

FAME AND CELEBRITY are alluring. People are drawn to those who walk in fame's spotlight, whether they are known for great accomplishments or for notorious deeds. The lives of the famous pique public interest and attract attention, perhaps because their experiences seem in some ways so different from, yet in other ways so similar to, our own.

Newspapers, magazines, and television regularly capitalize on this fascination with celebrity by running profiles of famous people. For example, television programs such as *Entertainment Tonight* devote all of their programming to stories about entertainment and entertainers. Magazines such as *People* fill their pages with stories of the private lives of famous people. Even newspapers, newsmagazines, and television news frequently delve into the lives of well-known personalities. Despite the number of articles and programs, few provide more than a superficial glimpse at their subjects.

Lucent's People in the News series offers young readers a deeper look into the lives of today's newsmakers, the influences that have shaped them, and the impact they have had in their fields of endeavor and on other people's lives. The subjects of the series hail from many disciplines and walks of life. They include authors, musicians, athletes, political leaders, entertainers, entrepreneurs, and others who have made a mark on modern life and who, in many cases, will continue to do so for years to come.

These biographies are more than factual chronicles. Each book emphasizes the contributions, accomplishments, or deeds that have brought fame or notoriety to the individual and shows how that person has influenced modern life. Authors portray their subjects in a realistic, unsentimental light. For example, Bill Gates—the cofounder and chief executive officer of the software giant Microsoft—has been instrumental in making personal computers the most vital tool of the modern age. Few dispute his business savvy, his perseverance, or his technical expertise, yet critics say he is ruthless in his dealings with competitors and driven more by his desire to maintain Microsoft's dominance in the computer industry than by an interest in furthering technology.

In these books, young readers will encounter inspiring stories about real people who achieved success despite enormous obstacles. Oprah Winfrey—the most powerful, most watched, and wealthiest woman on television today—spent the first six years of her life in the care of her grandparents while her unwed mother sought work and a better life elsewhere. Her adolescence was colored by promiscuity, pregnancy at age fourteen, rape, and sexual abuse.

Each author documents and supports his or her work with an array of primary and secondary source quotations taken from diaries, letters, speeches, and interviews. All quotes are footnoted to show readers exactly how and where biographers derive their information and provide guidance for further research. The quotations enliven the text by giving readers eyewitness views of the life and accomplishments of each person covered in the People in the News series.

In addition, each book in the series includes photographs, annotated bibliographies, timelines, and comprehensive indexes. For both the casual reader and the student researcher, the People in the News series offers insight into the lives of today's newsmakers—people who shape the way we live, work, and play in the modern age.

Introduction

Hollywood Rebel

After spending his earliest years in a small industrial town in Kentucky, Johnny Depp lived in more than thirty homes with his family before he was fifteen. Depp wanted to escape his unstable home life and become a rock star, and after a series of successful stints as a singer and guitarist performing as the opening act for top musicians, it seemed like his dream would come true. At age twenty, Depp moved to Los Angeles to pursue a music career, and while his band struggled to make it big, he turned to acting for extra money. Little did he know he would become one of the most critically acclaimed actors in Hollywood.

After playing small roles in several movies, Depp was cast as detective Tom Hanson in the popular television series *21 Jump Street*. The role propelled him to superstardom, and he became a reluctant teen heartthrob. After he left *Jump Street*, he set out to change his image by accepting offbeat and provocative movie roles. He became well known for playing emotionally troubled and eccentric characters as well as outcasts. His diverse résumé includes roles in comedies, dramas, and horror films, and he has portrayed romantic leads, action heroes, and villains.

By the early 1990s, Depp had built a solid career, but his personal life was markedly less stable. Depp had a series of high-profile romances and broken engagements. After his first marriage to makeup artist Lori Allison lasted only two years, Depp was linked to actresses Sherilyn Fenn, Jennifer Grey, and Winona Ryder, and model Kate Moss.

He also built a notorious reputation after a series of public scandals. His name became headline news in 1993 after actor

Johnny Depp feels his relationship with French celebrity Vanessa Paradis is responsible for much of his recent success.

River Phoenix died of a drug overdose at a club Depp co-owned. The following year, he was arrested for trashing a room at the Mark Hotel in New York City. Four years later he was in jail again, this time for threatening a crowd of paparazzi who wanted to photograph him for tabloid magazines. Depp did little to quell this image; in interviews, he freely discussed past drug use and self-destructive behavior.

Depp finally cleaned up his act after finding love with Vanessa Paradis, a French singer-actress he met in a Parisian pub. With a new role as a devoted boyfriend and father, he now lives with Paradis and their two children in the south of France. His new family gave him a new direction in life, and his career followed suit; since 1999 Depp has had some of the biggest successes of his career.

Depp endured a nomadic childhood as well as highly publicized breakups, drug problems, and legal troubles. However, through his remarkable professional and personal success, he has proven that no obstacles are too big for him to overcome.

Chapter 1

Wild Child

JOHN CHRISTOPHER DEPP II was born on June 9, 1963, in Owensboro, Kentucky, an industrial town located about one hundred miles southwest of Louisville. His family nicknamed him Johnny. He is the youngest of four children; his brother Danny is ten years his elder, his sister Debbie is seven years older, and his sister Christie is two years older. His father, John Christopher Depp, worked for the city as a civil engineer, and his mother, Betty Sue Depp, worked as a waitress.

Depp inherited Native American ancestry from both his mother and father. His maternal great-grandmother, Minnie, was a full-blooded Cherokee, and some of his paternal ancestors were also part Cherokee. Depp is a mixture of many other nationalities as well; he has Indian, Irish, and German ancestors.

Early Heartbreak

One of Depp's earliest memories was running around his family's backyard in July 1969 chasing lightning bugs with the young girl who lived next door. That night, he and the girl were swinging on a swing set when her father came outside to tell them that astronauts Neil Armstrong, Buzz Aldrin, and Michael Collins had landed on the moon. Depp was worried that something bad might happen when men walked on the moon. "I stayed up all night," he says. "It was a big relief when [the moon] didn't change."[1]

As a child, Depp spent much of his time picking tobacco on his grandfather's farm. Depp and his grandfather, whom he called Pawpaw, were inseparable. When his grandfather became ill,

Depp visited him often. Then, shortly after Depp's seventh birthday, his grandfather passed away. Depp was devastated; it was the first time he had lost someone so close to him. "That was a real big thing for me," Depp says. "But I'm sure my Pawpaw is around—guiding, watching."[2]

On the Move

Depp was still reeling from the death of his grandfather when his father announced the family would be moving from their home in Kentucky to Miramar, Florida. When they arrived in Florida, the family stayed in a hotel for almost a year while Depp's father searched for a job. He finally accepted a position as the director

Johnny Depp was born in a small industrial town in Kentucky. His father relocated the family to Florida when Depp was seven.

of public works in Miramar, and the family moved into a nearby apartment. Before Depp had a chance to adjust to the new home, however, his mother said they would be moving again.

It would not be the last time the family moved. Betty Sue was a free spirit who did not like to stay in one place for long. "We moved like gypsies,"[3] Depp says. Each time Depp settled into a new home, his family almost immediately packed their bags and moved again. Over the next few years, Depp's family lived in more than thirty different houses, sometimes staying in apartments, barns, or motels. One night, soon after Depp had adjusted to yet another new house, his parents announced they would be moving to the house next door. "I remember carrying my clothes across the yard and thinking, 'This is weird,'"[4] Depp says.

The constant moving took its toll on Depp, who was shy and had a hard time making new friends. His family moved several times each year, and he often had to start at a new school and find a new group of friends. Even when the family stayed in town, many of Depp's prized possessions got lost in the confusion of packing and relocating. "Little by little, all these things you saved . . . your football helmet or the drawings you made, they disappeared,"[5] he says. Depp never felt completely secure in any home because he knew that his family would soon be uprooted again. "To this day, I hate it when I have to move from location to location,"[6] he says.

Teenage Rebellion

As Johnny grew older, he became very close with his older brother, Danny. Often the brothers shared a bedroom wherever the family was staying. Danny loaned some of his favorite books and records to Johnny, who grew to love rock musicians Van Morrison and Bob Dylan and started collecting books by author Jack Kerouac. Depp was also obsessed with classic horror films, and as early as first grade, he would sit in class and draw pictures of Dracula and Frankenstein. His favorite TV show was a gothic soap opera called *Dark Shadows*, which often featured story lines about ghosts and werewolves. Depp was enthralled with the main character, Barnabas Collins, a vampire. Although his fascination with dark characters worried his parents, he watched every scary movie he could get his hands on.

As a child, Depp idolized Barnabas Collins, the vampire character on the gothic soap opera Dark Shadows.

It was not the only habit of Depp's that concerned his parents. As a child, he loved playing with Tinkertoys and Big Wheels, but as he grew older, he became more mischievous. Depp liked to play tricks on his family. His favorite prank was tape recording his family members simply because he enjoyed the idea that they did not know he was doing it.

He also came up with elaborate schemes; one day after watching someone on the TV show *Hogan's Heroes* dig a tunnel, he and a friend attempted to dig their own tunnel leading from Depp's bedroom to the backyard. When he developed a fascination with bugs and lizards, he imagined he could become an expert in training lizards and snakes. He caught chameleons in his yard and tried to train them to sit on his fingers.

Depp's activities soon became more dangerous. One of his idols when he was growing up was daredevil Robert "Evel"

Knievel, a stuntman who rode his motorcycle through walls of fire and jumped over cars, buses, and even mountain lions. Depp liked to try his own death-defying stunts, and he even dreamed up the perfect nickname for himself: Awful Knawful.

Like Knievel, who suffered several nasty spills and broke thirty-five bones in the course of his career, Depp's dangerous

Jack Kerouac

While he was growing up, one of Depp's literary heroes was Jack Kerouac. Kerouac, along with Allen Ginsberg, William S. Burroughs, and several of their acquaintants, was at the forefront of a literary movement known as the Beat generation. Kerouac coined the term *Beat* to express his feelings of disillusionment. His debut novel, *On the Road*, was published in 1957 and became the definitive novel of Beat literature.

Depp got the chance to portray Kerouac in the 1999 movie *The Source*, an independent documentary about Beat culture. As someone who had read Kerouac's novels since he was a teen and collected first editions of those novels as an adult, it was an extraordinary opportunity. Even though the movie was not widely released, Depp's performance was praised, and he was happy to have the chance to portray an author he admired.

Jack Kerouac, one of several disillusioned writers of the 1950s known as the Beat generation, is one of Depp's literary heroes.

feats sometimes caused him injury. One day while hanging out with a few friends, he decided to try to breathe fire like a circus performer. He wrapped a gasoline-soaked T-shirt around a pole, set the shirt on fire, then blew gasoline from his mouth. The flame ignited his eyebrows, and Depp ran screaming. One of his friends grabbed him and put out the fire: Depp bears a small scar on his right cheek from that incident. Still, he has never lost his adventurous streak, and like his daredevil idol, he continues to travel as much as possible by motorcycle.

Finding an Outlet

As Depp got older, his parents' marriage started to fall apart. They fought often, and the constant tension upset Depp. He tried to stay away from home and keep himself entertained as much as possible. That often meant breaking the law with his friends by stealing from nearby stores or breaking into his school and vandalizing classrooms. And when he was only eleven, Depp tried drugs for the first time. Still, he does not like to be thought of as a troublemaker. "It wasn't like I was some malicious kid,"[7] he says. Rather, his rebellious antics were his way of dealing with his unhappiness at home.

When Depp turned twelve, he found a more positive outlet for his frustration: music. His uncle was a preacher at a local church, and Depp attended his mass to watch the gospel choir perform. After watching one of the members of the choir play the electric guitar, Depp decided to try the instrument himself. He bought an electric guitar for twenty-five dollars, stole a chord book from a local department store, and spent hours in his room teaching himself how to play.

A few months later, he formed a band with a few other friends, and they started playing at backyard parties in their town. As the band became more popular, they were invited to perform at local clubs. Because Depp and his bandmates were underage, the club owners sneaked them in through the back door, and they had to leave immediately after playing the show. Nonetheless, Depp found he had easy access to alcohol and drugs from other clubgoers and started experimenting with various drugs. By the time he was fourteen years old, he was using drugs regularly. "Pretty much any drug you can name, I've done it,"[8] he says.

Depp soon realized that he did not want his drug use to interfere with his music career. "I looked around and said, 'This is not getting me anywhere,'"[9] he says. He stopped taking drugs and focused on his music instead, playing in more than fifteen bands while he was a teenager. He idolized rock musicians like Iggy Pop, Alice Cooper, and Aerosmith, and dreamed of someday becoming a rock star.

The more Depp got involved in music, the less he cared about school. Because Depp changed schools so often, he found it difficult to make friends or find a girlfriend. He was shy and felt like he did not fit in with his classmates. "I always felt like [a] total freak . . . that feeling of wanting to be accepted but not knowing how to be accepted as you are,"[10] he says. Most days, he skipped classes and went to the music class instead. The music teacher would give him a practice room, where he spent the day playing his guitar.

A Family Torn Apart

Meanwhile, his situation at home was steadily growing more difficult. His parents were still fighting, and the constant tension in the house worried Depp and his siblings. "It was rough," he says. "We grew up every day with the sense that something was about to blow."[11] Finally, when Depp was fifteen, his parents announced they were getting a divorce, and his father moved out of the house. Depp rarely saw his father after the divorce. Although Depp was slightly relieved that he would not have to hear his parents argue anymore, the news was still a shock. "I was thinking, 'Wait a minute, what happened to my family? What about stability, the safety of the home?'"[12] he says.

His mother had a difficult time dealing with the divorce. She fell ill soon after, and Depp blames her sudden sickness on her heartbreak. "Her life as she had known it for twenty years was over . . . her partner, her husband, her best friend, her lover, had just left her,"[13] Depp says. His sisters were both married and his brother had moved out, so Depp was alone in helping his mother recover in the next few months. During that time, he formed a bond with his mother that exists to this day. "She's just one of the smartest, funniest, greatest people I've ever been lucky enough to know," he says. "She's truly one of my best friends."[14]

Depp focused so much on making his mother happy that he was not able to deal with his own feelings about the divorce. "I didn't have time to mourn the loss of that sense of family, that sense of security,"[15] he says. Because he had assumed the role of caretaker, he felt like he had to be strong for his mother and could not grieve like a normal teenager might.

Depp was already having trouble dealing with authority at school, and his parents' divorce only made him more indignant. Disheartened, he dropped out of school and got a job pumping gas. Two weeks later, however, he returned to his high school. "I

Depp helped his mother Betty Sue to cope with her divorce from his father, and the two remain very close today.

A Friendship with Iggy Pop

Born James Newell Osterburg in 1947, Iggy Pop was one of Depp's musical idols. Like Depp, Pop got his start in a high school band called the Iguanas before joining a band called the Stooges as lead vocalist and guitarist. Pop eventually overcame a serious drug addiction, left the band, and released several solo albums that earned him the title "Godfather of Punk." He also pursued an acting career, playing small roles in fourteen movies and TV shows.

Depp had always admired Pop, and was thrilled to be able to work with him on several occasions. Pop had a small role in the movie *Cry-Baby*

and played Sally Jenko (a character named for Depp's best friend, Sal Jenco) in the 1996 western *Dead Man*. Pop also composed the music for *The Brave* and played an uncredited role in the film. Depp and Pop eventually formed a friendship based on their mutual admiration for each other.

A childhood idol of Depp's, punk rocker Iggy Pop has collaborated with Depp on several projects.

thought, 'This is crazy, I should go back,'"[16] he says. But because he had skipped so many classes, he had accumulated very few credits during his two years in high school. Rather than having him try to make up for lost time, the dean encouraged Depp to leave school and pursue his music career. Depp says the dean told him, "That's your passion, so you should go with that."[17]

Depp took the dean's advice and left school for good, but he worried about his future. His mother was still working as a waitress to support herself and him. At night he counted her tips for her, and some nights, after working a full ten-hour day, she earned only thirty dollars. Although Depp continued to perform at clubs with his band, the band earned very little money, so Depp worked at the gas station, too.

Once his mother had recovered, Depp started spending more time away from home. For awhile he stayed in his friend Sal Jenco's car because Jenco had nowhere else to live, and Depp did not want him to be lonely. However, living in Jenco's car reminded Depp of his nomadic childhood. He wanted a stable home, but at that point he had no clear direction in his life. He started to question his decision to leave high school and was afraid he would never accomplish anything. He even considered joining the marines; he thought it might give him some direction and help him learn to deal with authority. Before he could give the idea any serious thought, though, his band attained success.

Musical Dreams

Depp had been playing guitar with a rock group called The Kids, which played shows at local clubs in Florida. When Depp was seventeen, The Kids were invited to open a show in Florida for rock musician Iggy Pop. Depp was thrilled, as Pop had been one of his idols since he was young. After the show, Depp wanted to get Pop's attention, so he started yelling slurs and calling him names such as "Iggy Slop." Pop walked over to Depp, muttered an insult, and stormed away. Although it was not the most conventional way to approach someone, Depp was delighted that he had gotten a rise out of Pop.

As The Kids gained recognition, they were invited to open for other rock legends, including the Ramones, the Pretenders, Billy Idol, and the Talking Heads. An employee at The Palace, a concert venue in Hollywood, suggested that Depp and his band move to Los Angeles. Encouraged by their success, The Kids saved up their money. In 1983, when Depp was twenty, the band packed up and drove to California to pursue a record deal, sometimes driving for eighteen hours without sleeping. Despite the exhausting trip, Depp enjoyed the camaraderie of traveling with his bandmates.

When they arrived in Los Angeles, one of Depp's musician friends introduced him to a Hollywood makeup artist named Lori Allison. Depp and Allison started dating, and within a year they were married. Depp had found someone he truly loved to be with, and he was optimistic about the relationship. His music career, however, was becoming discouraging. The music scene in California was far more competitive than in Florida, and The Kids struggled to find even low-paying gigs at clubs around Los Angeles. "It was horrible," Depp says. "There were so many bands, it was impossible to make any money."[18]

Depp could not support himself and his new wife with the small amount of money he made as a musician, so he took a job as a telemarketer selling ballpoint pens over the phone. He disliked the job, and spent most of his time at work calling his mother long-distance from the company's phone. When his boss walked by, he would pretend he was taking a large order of pens; as soon as his boss passed, he would go back to chatting with his mom.

Although The Kids had been in Los Angeles for several months, they were still having trouble getting booked for shows, and they had no prospects for earning a record deal. Depp was struggling financially, and he did not know how he could pay his rent. However, his career was about to take an unexpected turn.

Chapter 2

A Change in Plans

W HILE THE KIDS played small shows around Los Angeles, Depp struggled to find a job with a solid income to support himself and his wife. Just as he was beginning to get discouraged, his wife introduced him to an aspiring actor named Nicolas Cage. Cage had appeared in several films, including *Valley Girl*, *Rumble Fish*, and *Cotton Club*. Depp was familiar with his work, and the two soon became close friends. Both were trying to build careers in Hollywood, and they often hung out at the local mall.

An Unexpected Chance

One day while Depp and Cage were walking down Melrose Avenue, Depp told Cage that he was having trouble finding a job. Cage suggested that Depp meet his agent and try to find some work as an actor. Depp figured that acting was a good way to pay his rent while the band waited for a record deal, and with no other job prospects in sight, he met with Cage's agent, Ilene Feldman.

Feldman was instantly impressed with Depp. "He's not what someone usually looks like when they're coming in to look for an agent, and that's what was so great about him,"[19] she says. She immediately arranged for Depp to audition for a horror movie called *A Nightmare on Elm Street*. Because Depp was a longtime fan of horror films, he readily agreed. She sent him to see director Wes Craven, who was casting actors for the movie.

Before Depp arrived, Craven had auditioned many actors who looked like typical California beach boys—blond, tan, and muscular. When Depp arrived at the casting, he immediately caught Craven's attention. With his dark hair, slim build, and unkempt appearance, he stood out from the other actors. Even though Depp was quiet, Craven could see that he was confident and charismatic; he did not try to impress Craven, but he was impressive anyway. "Johnny was more worldly, compared to all these pretty boys that were coming in,"[20] Craven says. After Craven had auditioned all the actors, he asked his teenage daughter and her friend which actor they liked best. Both of them voted for Depp, and Craven hired him for the role of Glen Lantz.

Depp had not expected anything to come of his audition, so he was pleasantly surprised to learn that Craven had chosen him for the part. "I was kind of excited," he says. "The possibility of being in a movie . . . the thought was miles away from anything I had ever dreamed of."[21]

A New Direction

Depp's role in *A Nightmare on Elm Street* was not exactly a standout part—the character Glen Lantz was one of the teens killed by a badly scarred figure who appears in their nightmares. Depp only had a few lines, and his character was murdered early in the movie.

Depp had no idea how to act; he had never even acted in a school play. He was surprised at how different performing in front of a movie camera was compared to performing with his band. When he was onstage, he could rely on his other band members to support him. If one member messed up in a song, the others could cover for him. When Depp was acting, however, his scenes depended entirely upon his own performance. He enjoyed the challenge and the twelve hundred dollars he earned each week of filming.

After *A Nightmare on Elm Street* finished filming, Depp went to see the movie. When he saw himself on the screen, he felt sick to his stomach. Seeing himself on an enormous movie screen made him uncomfortable, and the idea of thousands of people watching him die in a horror film was unsettling. Still, he was excited when the movie became a success, taking in $25 million at the box office and spawning an entire series of *Elm Street* movies.

By the time the filming of *Elm Street* ended, Depp's music career had stalled completely. Before he started filming the movie,

Nicolas Cage

Nicolas Cage, who befriended Depp and helped him start his acting career, was born into Hollywood royalty. The nephew of legendary filmmaker Francis Ford Coppola, Cage changed his name so he would not be accused of riding his uncle's coattails. Cage went on to play a number of neurotic and unstable characters and won over audiences as an unconventional leading man.

After Depp moved to Los Angeles, his girlfriend, Lori Allison, introduced him to Cage. They hit it off immediately. Both had dropped out of high school to pursue their career goals, and both actors had a rebellious side. They also had a lot in common when it came to romantic relationships; after Depp and Allison split up, she started dating Cage. Nonetheless, the two actors remained friends and have followed similar career paths. Like Depp, Cage has parlayed his fame as a teen sensation into one of the most diverse careers in Hollywood.

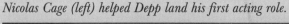

Nicolas Cage (left) helped Depp land his first acting role.

he knew the band's future was uncertain. After he put the band on hold for six weeks to film the movie, The Kids gave up and went their separate ways.

Without his band, Depp decided to put his musical career on hold indefinitely and pursue acting. After all, he had achieved more success with his first audition than he had in the past year with his band. Acting seemed more promising than music. "I seemed to be having more steam with acting,"[22] he says.

Shortly after he decided to pursue acting wholeheartedly, Depp earned a lead role in another movie, a racy teen comedy called *Private Resort*. In it, he played Jack, one of two teenage boys who spent the weekend chasing girls at a Florida resort. His costar was an actor from New York City named Rob Morrow, and Depp and Morrow both loved pulling pranks. After filming ended, Depp and Morrow wanted to see the test screening, where the movie is shown to a small audience who give feedback and critique. No one involved with the movie was allowed to attend the test screening, but Depp and Morrow fashioned disguises so they could sneak in. Depp wore thick glasses and a knit hat, and Morrow put cotton in his mouth to puff out his cheeks. They walked past all the executives from the movie studio and watched the screening.

Depp's first lead role was in Private Resort *(pictured is a promotional poster), a commercial and critical flop.*

Spend a weekend with no reservations!

PRIVATE RESORT

They're looking for hot times. And they came to the right place...

Private Resort

A String of Disappointments

Private Resort was a commercial and critical failure. Depp was not happy with the finished product and thought his performance could have been better. Before he looked for other roles, he wanted to refine his acting skills. He enrolled in acting classes and studied with acting coach Peggy Feury at the Loft Studio in Los Angeles. When he was not at the studio, he read books on acting technique. One book about method acting called *No Acting, Please*, changed his view on the craft. It explained that actors should not *play* a character; instead, they should *become* a character. Depp would ultimately become widely recognized for his unmatched ability to take on a character's personality.

He looked for more acting jobs but was having trouble finding roles in major motion pictures. In 1985, he made guest appearances on two television shows and appeared in a made-for-television crime drama called *Slow Burn* in which he played a teenager who was being tracked by a private investigator. The movie received very little attention, and Depp started to wonder if his acting career was as promising as it had initially seemed.

That same year, his marriage to Allison ended. Depp knew that he and Allison were no longer right for each other, but because he had been traumatized by his parents' divorce, he tried to save his own marriage. For a while he tried to deny that he was no longer in love. "I was forcing myself into a situation where [I was thinking], 'It could have been love,'"[23] he says.

For a short time, it seemed like nothing was going smoothly in Depp's life. Then he auditioned for a role in the emotional 1985 war drama *Platoon*. Directed by legendary director and former Vietnam War soldier Oliver Stone, the movie centered around a new recruit in the Vietnam War who faced a moral dilemma when one of his sergeants ordered the troop to burn down a village. Although Depp was nervous when auditioning for the highly acclaimed director, Stone was impressed with Depp and offered him the role of Lerner, an interpreter.

Depp spent three months filming in the Philippines. Stone required all the actors to go through basic training under the supervision of a military adviser to give them an idea of what it was like to be a soldier in the Vietnam War. Depp and the other actors

barely slept during the intense physical training. By the time filming started, they were exhausted, which suited their war-weary
characters perfectly.

Although the training was challenging, filming *Platoon* gave
Depp the chance to work with and learn from accomplished actors like Willem Dafoe and Forest Whitaker. Depp assumed appearing in such a highly regarded film would help bring him into
the spotlight. When the movie was released, however, many of
Depp's scenes had been cut.

Even so, starring in the movie had been an invaluable experience. *Platoon* grossed more than $150 million worldwide. It was
nominated for several Oscars, won the Academy Award for Best
Picture in 1986, and was named one of the American Film
Institute's 100 Greatest Movies of All Time. Although Depp's role
was minor, appearing in such an acclaimed movie gave him pres-
tige, and suddenly studio executives saw him as a serious actor.

Breakout Role

Depp's performance caught the attention of television executive
Patrick Hasburgh, who was developing a series about a group of
police officers who worked undercover in high schools. The show
was called *21 Jump Street*, and Hasburgh offered Depp the role of
Tom Hanson. Depp was still interested in movie roles and did not
want the time commitment of filming a weekly television series,
so he turned down the part. The network hired actor Jeff Yagher
to play the role instead.

Depp continued to audition for movies but was getting discouraged because no one had sent him any good scripts. He was
broke, so for a while he stayed in Nicolas Cage's one-room apartment. At one point, Depp was so poor that he stole Mexican pe-
sos from Cage's drawer and had them exchanged into American
currency at a check-cashing store just to support himself. Years
later, at an awards ceremony, Depp admitted to Cage that he had
stolen money from him when he ran into financial problems. Cage
quickly forgave his friend; he, too, remembered what it had been
like to struggle as an actor in Los Angeles.

Just as Depp was starting to lose hope, Hasburgh contacted
him again. Hasburgh knew Depp had been disappointed when

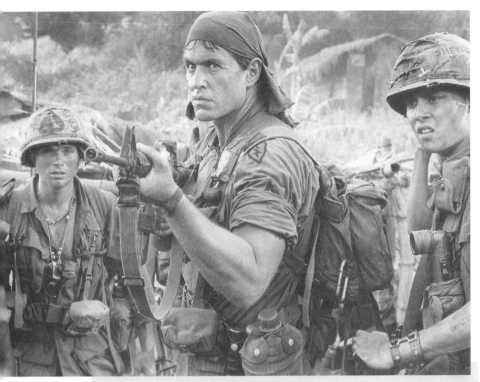

Depp's small part in the Oscar-winning film Platoon *established him as a serious Hollywood actor.*

his scenes were cut from *Platoon*, and he was aware that Depp had not found any significant movie roles since. Because Yagher was not working out in the role of Hanson, Hasburgh offered Depp a second chance to accept the role. If Depp accepted, he would sign a six-year contract and be paid forty-five thousand dollars per episode.

As Depp thought about the opportunity, he realized that taking on the role would guarantee him a steady paycheck for at least a season. In addition, because many television shows are canceled after the first season, he assumed that he would not be obligated to the show for an extended period.

Depp felt the show had a lot of potential and that it addressed some important issues, so he finally agreed to audition for the role. The producers liked him instantly: "He had this presence,"[24] says supervising producer Steve Beers. Depp moved to Vancouver,

Depp (right) quickly emerged as the star of the television series 21 Jump Street. *His handsome looks helped the show draw large numbers of young viewers.*

British Columbia, to film *21 Jump Street*, and the producers retaped the pilot with Depp in the role of Hanson. Laid-back, self-assured, and polite to everyone on the set, he immediately clicked with the other cast members.

Not wanting to be alone in an unfamiliar town, Depp convinced his mother and her new husband, Robert Palmer, to move to Vancouver to keep him company during the nine months a year that *Jump Street* taped. He also invited his friend Jenco to visit him on the set often. When Jenco showed producers his bizarre ability to puff out his cheeks like a blowfish, they offered him a recurring role as a minor character named Blowfish.

A Surprise Hit

When *21 Jump Street* first aired, it placed only 140th out of 163 shows in the Nielsen ratings, a list of most watched shows in television. Despite the low ratings, the show generated a lot of hype. To Depp's surprise, much of that hype centered around him. He was considered to be the star of the show, and many viewers who had not previously been familiar with his work were instantly

The Life of James Dean

In his early career, Depp was often compared to the fast-living, rebellious heartthrob James Dean. Born February 8, 1931, Dean was raised on an Indiana farm before moving to California to attend college. There he enrolled in an acting workshop and appeared in several television commercials. In 1951, he moved to New York to pursue an acting career. He was an instant success, earning several major roles in TV shows and Broadway plays.

In 1955, Dean moved back to Hollywood where he went on to star in three movies: *East of Eden, Giant*, and his most famous work, the 1955 film *Rebel Without a Cause*. His restless, rebellious image earned him a devoted fan base. He was even nominated for two Academy Awards that year, for *Giant* and *Rebel Without a Cause*, but he never lived to see the nominations. On September 30, 1955, Dean drove his new Porsche

to a racing event in Salinas. Speeding along the highway at 115 miles an hour, Dean was killed in a head-on collision. He had only been in Hollywood for a year, but the outpouring of grief showed just how much he had accomplished in his twenty-four years.

Early in his acting career, Depp was often compared to the rebellious James Dean.

intrigued. Often compared to the late actor James Dean, Depp was unlike any other actor on television at the time. He was dark, brooding, and had a natural charisma. "Everybody else tries to be cool, but Johnny just *is*,"[25] says his *Jump Street* costar, Holly Robinson Peete.

Producers felt that Depp's handsome looks could attract more viewers to the series, so they expected him to take on the responsibility of promoting the show. Because Depp had long hair and often wore grungy clothes, they stereotyped him as a rebellious teen idol and instructed him to uphold that image. Depp did not agree with that description, and he certainly did not feel comfortable exploiting that image as a way of promoting the series.

In order to garner more interest in the show, network executives planned a tour in which the cast members would visit schools in several cities around the United States and talk to students about the dangers of drug use. Depp disliked all the attention he was getting in the media, and he was uncomfortable with the idea of lecturing students on drug use as a way to sell the TV show.

At first it seemed as though Depp would back out of the tour completely, but the night before their first scheduled appearance in Chicago, Illinois, Depp took a late-night flight and arrived in time to meet the other cast members the next morning. That day, at the school, he told students to stay in school and say no to drugs. He felt the underlying message of the show—which addressed the problem of teenage drug use—was a good one, and in the end, it was important to him to get that message across to his audience. "Drugs are the worst," he said. "I just tell people to stay far away."[26]

Depp and the cast were invited to a "Just Say No" event at the White House. At that time, Ronald Reagan was president, and First Lady Nancy Reagan had started the "Just Say No" program to educate students about the dangers of drugs. Depp brought his mother to the event, and they spent the day people watching at the swanky affair.

Depp may have been reluctant to do the tour, but it generated interest in the show among young viewers. As word spread

Depp Gives Back

Depp does not take his success for granted, and from his first moments of fame, he has tried to give back as much as possible. He started working with the Make-a-Wish Foundation in 1987, just after he got his big break on *21 Jump Street*, visiting terminally ill children or bringing them onto movie sets to hang out with him. "The most courageous people I've met have been nine years old," he told *Premiere* magazine in December 1999. "The strength that they have—that's some kind of strength." He has been involved with the organization ever since.

Depp also holds charity events at his club, the Viper Room, and has raised tens of thousands of dollars for the Starlight Foundation, another organization that helps terminally ill children. In 1995, he played guitar on a benefit album to raise funds for orphans of the Bosnian war. Depp also tries to be charitable in his everyday life, whether leaving generous tips at restaurants or handing out food and money to the homeless.

about *21 Jump Street*, the show climbed in the ratings, and it was renewed for a second and third season. Depp's photo was plastered across the pages of teen magazines. Television commercials for *Jump Street* capitalized on Depp's newfound status as a teen idol, and he even saw one commercial for the show in which he was the only cast member mentioned. Soon he was receiving ten thousand letters a month, and fans were stopping him on the street to beg for an autograph or picture.

Trying to Escape

Depp was uncomfortable with his sudden stardom, and he found the attention unnerving. He wanted to be taken seriously as an actor, so he did not like the idea of being packaged as a heartthrob. "I was without question a product," Depp says. "It was a very uncomfortable situation."[27] Whether or not Depp wanted the attention, though, it was unavoidable.

Depp was also starting to have deeper concerns about the show. He felt that his character was arrogant and hypocritical and once said the only thing he had in common with Hanson was his physical appearance. Although Depp had been happy with the story lines and the serious issues addressed early in the show's history, he did not like the direction the show took in its third season. He felt the stories had become too unrealistic, and he worried that the show was glamorizing crime. Several times he refused to act in an episode because he did not approve of the way it handled a topic. In one episode, Depp's character denies he is an undercover police officer; later, a student is murdered after his classmates suspect *he* is the undercover cop. Depp did not like the idea of his character being indirectly responsible for a student's death. When he backed out of the episode, actor Richard Greico was hired to fill in for him. From that point on, whenever Depp did not feel comfortable with a plot, he forfeited his salary for that episode, and Greico stepped in as a character named Detective Booker.

Depp desperately wanted to be released from his contract. He was so eager to leave that he even tried to strike a deal with the show's producers: He would film one more season of the show without pay on the grounds that he could be released from the contract at the end of the season. The producers did not accept the offer; they knew Depp was one of the main reasons viewers tuned in to the show each week.

As Depp continued to plead with the studio to release him from the show, he gained a reputation for being difficult to work with. He tried to annoy the producers so they would fire him, and sometimes his schemes reflected his offbeat sense of humor: Once, he stubbornly insisted that his character should develop an obsession with peanut butter. Tabloids reported that Depp had thrown tantrums on the set, and some even suggested that he had physically attacked the show's producers.

Depp thought the rumors were ridiculous. Although he admitted that he had declined to appear in episodes he did not approve of, he maintained that he was never violent on set. According to Depp, his willingness to speak his mind and stand up for his beliefs had unfairly earned him a reputation as an on-set bully.

Even though he was uncomfortable with his sudden fame and disliked the direction that *21 Jump Street* had taken, Depp was grateful to have steady work in a competitive field. "They gave me a job, they gave me a paycheck, and they put me on the map,"[28] he says. Although it was not an ideal situation for him, working on *21 Jump Street* gave Depp financial freedom and the exposure he needed to land movie roles. He was now a household name, and movie studios were eager to cast him in leading roles.

Depp had decided, however, that he no longer wanted to be a teen idol. He worried that his heartthrob label would cause movie producers to stereotype him. Instead, Depp wanted to choose roles that challenged people's expectations. This decision would define his career in the years to come.

Chapter 3

Finding His Niche

Depp was determined to change his reputation. He searched for more substantial roles that would allow him to be seen as a serious actor rather than a teen idol. Over the next few years, he would choose diverse and unconventional roles, which helped him cement his status as a reputable character actor.

Although his career was improving, Depp was having difficulties in his personal life. He was disturbed to find that his sudden fame with *21 Jump Street* had taken away his privacy. While working on the show, Depp began dating actress Sherilyn Fenn and the couple were engaged briefly. Depp chose not to share the details of his love life with the media and did not want to talk publicly about his relationship. Despite his wishes, reporters attempted to uncover the details of their romance and tried to snap pictures of the couple together.

He and Fenn split soon after becoming engaged, but when he started dating actress Jennifer Grey shortly thereafter, the media frenzy started up again. He and Grey also became engaged, but both actors were very busy with their careers and they rarely had time to see each other. Depp was filming *21 Jump Street* in Vancouver, and Grey was working in Los Angeles. When they split in 1989, Depp declined to talk about the reasons for their breakup, but their friends said the long-distance relationship was too difficult to maintain. Depp was again surprised to see that it became a hot topic of gossip. "If people want to sit around and talk about who I've dated, then I'd say they have a lot of spare time and should consider other topics,"[29] he said.

Laughing at Labels

Once his relationship with Grey ended, Depp shifted his focus back to his career. After three years on *21 Jump Street*, there was still no end in sight for the series. Depp had signed on for six years, and it seemed as though he would be forced to fulfill the contract. He understood that he was legally bound to appear on the show and he intended to abide by the contract, but he also continued to pursue movie roles.

In 1990, director John Waters offered him a role in his musical romantic comedy *Cry-Baby*, a spoof of movies like *Grease*. He cast Depp to play Wade "Cry-Baby" Walker, a juvenile delinquent who falls for a virtuous rich girl. As soon as Depp read three pages of the movie script, he knew it was a part he had to play.

The over-the-top movie poked fun at clichéd "rebel" and "goody-goody" stereotypes, and it carried a message that people should not be judged based on the labels they are given. Depp was instantly attracted to that concept. The movie was not a major commercial success, but Depp liked that his character parodied his own reputation for being a brooding rebel. "One of the

The role of Wade "Cry-Baby" Walker in the film Cry-Baby *allowed Depp to spoof his own reputation as a teen rebel.*

reasons I did [*Cry-Baby*] is that . . . it really made fun of what people's idea of me was,"[30] Depp says.

Shortly after he finished filming *Cry-Baby*, a friend introduced Depp to eighteen-year-old actress Winona Ryder. Depite the eight-year age difference, Depp and Ryder hit it off and began dating soon after they met. "We just started hanging out, and we've been hanging out ever since," Depp later said. "I love her more than anything in the world."[31] Depp was so smitten, he got a tattoo on his shoulder that read, "Winona Forever." As a gift, Ryder bought Depp a star in the sky from the International Star Registry and named it after him. "From what I know, it looks exactly like me,"[32] Depp joked.

Dream Role

Depp was finally feeling more content. Then he received the news he had been awaiting for more than three years: His agents had found a loophole in his contract, and he was going to be released from *21 Jump Street*. He filmed his final episode in the middle of the show's fourth season. Depp said of a future commitment to a television series: "I would never do it again. There's not enough money in Los Angeles."[33]

Just when it seemed things could not get any better for Depp, he was offered a chance to play the title role in director Tim Burton's new movie, a gothic love story called *Edward Scissorhands*. Burton had recently been praised for his dark comedy *Beetlejuice*, in which Ryder had starred, and Depp respected Burton's work. When Depp read the script for *Edward Scissorhands*, he was immediately impressed. "It was really like great literature," he says. "It was a once-in-a-lifetime thing."[34]

Edward Scissorhands is the story of a young man created by a mad scientist. When the scientist dies before the creation is complete, Edward is left with scissors for his hands. He lives alone in an old mansion until a woman discovers him and brings him home with her where he falls in love with her daughter Kim. The other people in the neighborhood have trouble accepting Edward into their community, however, and he is often cruelly taunted.

It was a touching script, and Depp had stiff competition for the role. Although the movie was very different from the usual

Winona Ryder

Although Winona Ryder's relationship with Johnny Depp ended in heart-break, the two have shared a similar career path, earning critical acclaim while enduring tabloid scrutiny. When Depp and Ryder began dating, Depp was still an up-and-coming star, but Ryder was already a Hollywood veteran. At the age of fourteen, she earned her first role in the movie *Lucas*, but her breakthrough came when she played a suicidal teen who hangs out with ghosts in her attic in the 1988 comedy *Beetlejuice*. After she and Depp appeared together in *Edward Scissorhands*, she went on to play dark, often disturbing roles in movies like *Heathers, Bram Stoker's Dracula*, and *Girl, Interrupted*. Like Depp, Ryder prefers playing characters who are outcasts or eccentrics rather than typical romantic leads. Critics have praised her performances, and she earned an Oscar nomination for her role in the 1993 drama *The Age of Innocence*.

Ryder understood Depp's difficult childhood. Ryder was raised in a hippie commune and had to be home-schooled after classmates teased her for her boyish appearance. Ryder has also had her share of controversy. While dating Depp, she checked herself into a hospital because she was suffering from depression and anxiety attacks. In December 2001, two

years after Depp made headlines for threatening a photographer, Ryder was arrested in Beverly Hills for allegedly shoplifting several thousand dollars worth of merchandise from the upscale department store Saks Fifth Avenue. She was found guilty of vandalism and grand theft in November 2002, and sentenced to community service. Nonetheless, her talent has outshined her scandals and she continues to enjoy a successful film career.

One of Depp's former girlfriends, Winona Ryder enjoys a successful acting career despite the controversy in her life.

romantic comedies, many actors were interested in the role because it was so unique. Well-known celebrities like Tom Hanks, Tom Cruise, and Michael Jackson were reportedly interested in playing Edward. Depp was so intimidated that he was reluctant to meet with Burton.

As soon as Burton met Depp, though, he knew Depp would be the ideal actor to portray Edward. The character had very little dialogue during the movie, and Burton felt that Depp could convey a deep sense of emotion through his eyes. The director knew Depp was uncomfortable with fame and could relate to Edward's fear of being judged. Burton, believing Depp was perfect for Edward, gave him the role.

Then Burton cast Ryder as Depp's costar and Edward's love interest. The year before, while Depp was dating Grey, he had learned how difficult it could be to maintain a relationship when both people were working as actors. But with Ryder as his costar,

Depp's role as Edward Scissorhands in the successful film of the same name established the actor as a Hollywood star.

Depp would not have to spend time away from her while he filmed. He was excited to work with her. "She has a lot of talent and, aside from that, I also happen to love her," he said. "I'm sure we're going to do more things together."[35]

Depp's Big Break

The shoot was difficult at times. Depp often stood outside in stifling heat for hours, dressed in Edward's trademark black leather. He also had to learn to function with scissor blades attached to his hands, because he could not always remove them between scenes. And even after earning the role, Depp worried that he would be replaced. He was relaxing in his room one day when he heard a knock at the door. Two young girls were there, and Depp assumed they had come to ask him for his autograph. Instead, the girls asked if Tom Hanks lived there. Depp panicked. "I was *convinced* that Hanks would be replacing me,"[36] he says.

Depp proved to be irreplaceable as Edward. He immediately felt a connection to his character. "There's quite a lot of Edward in me, and a lot of me in him,"[37] he says. The movie is touching and at times heartbreaking, and Depp quickly realized it would have a strong emotional impact. Before the film was released, he attended a scoring session in which an orchestra records the music for the film. As soon as the orchestra played the first notes of the *Edward Scissorhands* theme, Depp was so moved that tears streamed down his face.

Edward Scissorhands proved to be Depp's breakthrough role. Audiences were drawn to his emotional portrayal of Edward, and Hollywood executives were impressed that Depp, dressed in a fright wig, white makeup, and bladed hands, could still play a character that was undeniably human. Audiences related to Edward, and Depp received critical acclaim as a character actor. Although the movie received very little attention in its first weekend, it quickly gained word-of-mouth recognition and ultimately brought in more than $53 million at the box office.

Negative Attention

Depp was suddenly the talk of Hollywood, but not all the attention was positive. He and Ryder had always talked openly about their romance, and he feels that the lack of privacy hurt their relationship. Tabloids often published rumors and gossip about them, which made it difficult for them to have a normal relationship. They started to drift apart and eventually went their separate ways.

Depp's "Winona Forever" tattoo had proven to be far more permanent than his relationship with Ryder, but at first, Depp did not want to get the tattoo removed. He thought of his tattoos as a way of keeping a journal and marking important events in his life, so removing the tattoo would be akin to pretending the relationship had never happened. Eventually, though, he decided to undergo a procedure called dermabrasion, in which pulses of light are aimed at the skin to break down the tattoo pigment so the body can absorb it naturally. The procedure is expensive and extremely painful, so Depp decided to remove the tattoo one letter at a time. For a brief time, the tattoo famously read "Wino Forever."

Depp also endured criticism for his grungy appearance. He was not concerned with fashion, and usually dressed in ripped jeans, tattered T-shirts, and knit caps pulled over his unkempt hair. As a result, in 1993 he was named one of *People* magazine's worst-dressed celebrities. Depp was not insulted at all: "As far as being one of the worst dressed, I was *proud*," he says. "My goal is to be number one worst dressed."[38]

Meanwhile, Depp was getting positive buzz for a new business venture. Along with Los Angeles–based musician Chuck E. Weiss and Depp's best friend Jenco, Depp purchased a nightclub called the Viper Room on the famed Sunset Strip in West Hollywood. Depp wanted to bring back the culture of 1930s Hollywood and offer a place where people could hang out with friends and listen to great music. On opening night, Tom Petty played a benefit show at the club that raised close to fifteen thousand dollars for a charity called the Starlight Foundation. Often, top-name artists would perform at the Viper Room before embarking on national tours; some musicians who performed there were Johnny Cash, Bruce Springsteen, Iggy Pop, Lenny Kravitz, and Sheryl Crow. The club received a lot of hype, not just because of its famous owners but also because of its relaxed, stylish atmosphere.

Depp's Musical Career

In addition to running the Viper Room, Depp continued to enjoy playing music as a hobby. While he was filming a movie in Texas, he and Jenco met two local musicians, songwriter Bill Carter and Butthole Surfers singer Gibby Haynes. The four musicians hung out together, cooking gourmet meals and talking about music. Eventually they decided to start a rock band, which they named P.

P released its debut album in 1995 featuring guest appearances by Red Hot Chili Peppers' bassist Flea and Sex Pistols' guitarist Steve Jones. Despite the all-star musical lineup, many critics questioned whether or not a movie star could produce a "real" rock record. In the end, the album was solid and received many positive reviews, but the band members were not concerned with critical success or commercial appeal. They just wanted to have fun and make

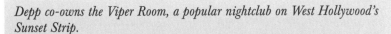

Depp co-owns the Viper Room, a popular nightclub on West Hollywood's Sunset Strip.

music. Although P never officially toured and never released a follow-up album, the band played occasional gigs at the Viper Room. Depp appeared in the music video for Tom Petty's hit "Into the Great Wide Open" and went on to play guitar on two Oasis albums. Although he has not had the same success with music as he has with acting, it continues to be one of his greatest passions.

Diverse Choices

In 1993, Depp took on two more movie roles that allowed him to play unique and unusual characters. First he was offered a part in director Emir Kusturica's drama *Arizona Dream*. Depp and Kusturica had clashed at their first meeting to discuss the film, so Depp told his agent he did not want to do the movie. Then, about a month later, Kusturica asked to meet with Depp again. This time they hit it off, and Depp accepted the role. Depp played Axel, a young man who falls for an eccentric widow and then later becomes romantically involved with her equally strange daughter. Although the movie was not a major release, it earned Depp critical acclaim for his role. His costar, Vincent Gallo, was impressed with Depp's ability to appeal to audiences without taking on typical male leads. "[He has] been able to permeate the mainstream without pandering to it,"[39] Gallo says.

Depp then accepted a starring role in the film *Benny & Joon.* In the popular romantic comedy, a young man hires a caretaker to watch over his mentally disturbed sister, Joon. Depp plays Sam, the man who signs on to look after Joon and eventually falls in love with her. Their romance helps Joon overcome her emotional problems.

Depp gained the respect of his costars during filming. Mary Stuart Masterson, who played Joon, said, "He makes bold choices . . . I think people appreciate that."[40] He also earned a reputation as a caring, considerate person to work with. Once when a crew member complained that he missed good pizza, Depp had thirty pizzas flown in from Los Angeles to the movie set in Spokane, Washington, for him.

The movie was lauded by critics, some of whom compared Depp's quirky character nuances to those of a classic silent-movie star. He communicated most of his thoughts and feelings through facial expressions and gestures. His wardrobe in the movie was also reminiscent of old-fashioned films; he wore a top hat and tuxedo jacket through much of the film. The role cemented Depp's status as a character actor, someone who plays offbeat or eccentric characters rather than conventional lead roles.

Depp's Feminine Side

In 1994, Depp began filming a biographical movie about Edward D. Wood, a director who was widely known as the worst director of all time. Depp had met with Burton at a café in Hollywood where Burton explained the idea for *Ed Wood*. He had barely spoken for five minutes when Depp agreed to take on the lead role. "I was like, 'Okay, let's do it, I'm there. Just say when,'"[41] he says.

The role required Depp to wear an interesting costume. Because Wood often dressed in women's clothing, Depp had to wear angora sweaters and high heels on set. He even spent several days wearing a tight girdle. He said the role helped him get in touch with his feminine side, deepened his respect for women, and gave him a newfound appreciation for the trouble women go through to be fashionable. "I have a tremendous respect for women. I love women—and I hate angora sweaters,"[42] he says.

Proving His Devotion

Depp's dedication to the role of Wood was apparent to everyone who knew him. Depp was normally known for his quiet demeanor and dark sense of humor, but Wood was eternally upbeat and optimistic. During the nine months Depp spent filming the movie, he adopted Wood's jovial personality even after he left the set. He was so deeply committed to the character that his friends often had to remind him to relax and act like himself.

On the set, Depp once again demonstrated the helpful, outgoing nature he was known for. "He's the star, but he's always running around asking if you need water or anything,"[43] said Depp's costar Sarah Jessica Parker. Depp would even ask the crew members if they needed help carrying the cable.

He also helped one of his costars through a troubling incident: On Patricia Arquette's first day of filming, one of the extras in a

The Legend of Tim Burton

Depp has worked with director Tim Burton on three films, and Burton is one of Depp's favorite directors. Like Depp, Burton spent most of his childhood watching horror films. After working as an apprentice for Disney animation, Burton made his directorial debut with the offbeat comedy *Pee-Wee's Big Adventure*. The film was a huge hit in the 1980s, as was Burton's second effort, the creepy comedy *Beetlejuice*. He was hired as the director for the big-screen version of *Batman* in 1989 before going on to direct Depp's 1990 breakout role in *Edward Scissorhands*.

Since then, Burton has continued to attract audiences with his darkly funny, often twisted movies. He has had several more major successes with *The Nightmare Before Christmas*, *Batman Forever*, *Sleepy Hollow*, and *Planet of the Apes*, and in 2003 was developing a remake of *Charlie and the Chocolate Factory* in which Depp hopes to appear as Willy Wonka.

Tim Burton (right) is one of Depp's favorite directors and the two have worked on several projects together.

wedding scene started to act hostile. Between takes, the extra screamed insults at Arquette and even threatened to kill herself. Depp was able to pacify the girl by talking to her quietly. After all, it was similar to the incident at the nightclub years before when Depp insulted Iggy Pop just to get a reaction from his idol. If anyone could relate to her, it was Depp.

Though *Ed Wood* was not a major commercial success, it received excellent reviews, and Depp's portrayal of the eccentric director was dead-on. Depp captured Wood's enthusiasm and zany spirit perfectly, and the role showcased his ability to make audiences relate to his eccentric characters. But over the next few years, a series of public scandals would overshadow his talent, and Depp would have to fight to bring his acting ability back to the forefront.

Chapter 4

Hard Times

IT SEEMED DEPP'S career was going smoothly, and the Viper Room quickly became a popular Hollywood hangout. The laid-back atmosphere in the club meant that celebrities could relax without being bothered by fans, and consequently many A-list actors and musicians visited on a regular basis. Then a tragedy at the club tarnished Depp's image and sent him spiraling into destructive drug use.

Tragedy at the Viper Room

On the eve of Halloween in 1993, patrons, many of them dressed in wild costumes, packed into the club for a Halloween party. Shortly before 1:00 A.M., someone was found in the bathroom shaking uncontrollably. It was River Phoenix, a free-spirited actor who had gained popularity with several highly acclaimed

River Phoenix, a talented young actor, overdosed on drugs at Depp's Viper Room. The death of his friend devastated Depp.

movie roles. Several other clubgoers helped Phoenix outside to calm him down, but he collapsed on the sidewalk and went into convulsions. While his sister, Rain, tried to stop his seizures, his brother, Joaquin, called for an ambulance. By the time Phoenix arrived at Cedars-Sinai Medical Center, he had gone into full cardiac arrest. At 1:51 A.M., he was pronounced dead. Although few of his fans even realized he was involved with drugs, doctors ruled that Phoenix had overdosed on a combination of heroin and cocaine.

Depp cried upon hearing there had been a death at his club. When he heard it was his friend River Phoenix, he was devastated. The loss of Phoenix was extremely difficult for Depp. "It was just a nightmare you never recover from," he says. "What a waste of a talented, beautiful guy."[44] Depp barely had time to mourn, however. The next day, news of Phoenix's death was splashed across the newspapers, and it seemed that every report mentioned Depp's name. Some reports even indirectly blamed Depp, suggesting that he allowed patrons to use drugs at his club. Depp was infuriated that the media would hold him responsible.

Getting Back to Work

Depp still had movie obligations to fulfill, and soon after Phoenix's death, he started filming a drama called *What's Eating Gilbert Grape*. In the movie, Depp plays Gilbert, a young man who spends all

In What's Eating Gilbert Grape, *Depp (right) plays the role of Gilbert, a young man who spends his time caring for his obese mother and retarded brother.*

his time taking care of his obese mother and mentally disabled brother, Arnie. He believes he must abandon his own dreams to take care of his family, until he starts a romance with a worldly traveler named Becky who helps him rethink his life. Depp was immediately drawn to Gilbert, a quiet character with a wide range of emotions. "I was intrigued by this guy, not by what he said, but by what he didn't say."[45]

The shoot proved to be the most difficult one of Depp's career. He was depressed and found it difficult to stay focused. He could not stop thinking about Phoenix's death, and the tabloids offered a constant reminder of what had happened. Also, playing the role of Gilbert brought back upsetting memories from Depp's own childhood. Like Gilbert, Depp felt like he had lost part of his childhood by spending his teen years taking care of his mother instead of being a carefree kid. "It's always taxing to play something that's closer to reality,"[46] Depp says. Then, in January 1994, Depp's Los Angeles home was destroyed in an earthquake. Without a permanent residence, Depp spent the next few months living in the Chateau Marmont and Hollywood Roosevelt hotels until he could find a new home.

Eventually it became too much for Depp to bear, and he turned to drugs to help him escape his grief. He drank heavily, slept rarely, and relied on drugs to dull his pain. "I numbed myself and poisoned myself for so many years, only to find out that it's really selfish and really dumb,"[47] he says.

While he was on set, however, Depp was professional and pleasant to work with. "There's an element of Johnny that's extremely nice, and extremely cool, but at the same time, he's hard to figure out," said his costar, Leonardo DiCaprio, who played Arnie. "But that's what makes him interesting."[48] Depp's performance was poignant, likely because it was so easy for him to relate to the troubled character.

Falling Apart

Off the set, Depp seemed unbalanced. In 1994, he was invited to introduce Neil Young at the Oscars, but he panicked before going onstage. Instead of reading his lines from the teleprompter, he hastily introduced Young and then hurried off the stage. He rushed outside in the middle of the ceremony and begged Harrison Ford's limo driver to take him back to his hotel.

Depp talked openly in interviews about his self-destructive behavior. He has a series of scars on his left arm; he explained that he cut himself to mark important events in his life and compared the slices to getting a tattoo. When Depp admitted to his self-mutilation, the incident at the Viper Room was still making headlines in the tabloids, and this disclosure did little to improve his tarnished reputation.

His behavior was becoming increasingly destructive. He was using drugs frequently and eventually reached a point where he was going days at a time without food or sleep, subsisting mainly on coffee. One day while sitting around with a group of friends, his unhealthy habits caught up to him. Although he was not using drugs at the time, his heart started racing, and no matter how hard he tried to calm down, he could not get it to slow down. Finally his friend rushed him to the hospital where he was given a shot that stopped his heart for a brief second. His heartbeat returned to normal, but the incident was enough to scare Depp into shape.

Depp knew he needed to clean up his act, so he stopped doing drugs and spent the next nine months focusing on his movie career and trying to stay out of trouble. For a while it seemed as though Depp's troubled reputation was behind him for good.

Ups and Downs

In 1994, Depp fell in love once again, this time with British supermodel Kate Moss. Depp and Moss met in February 1994 at Café Tabac, a trendy spot in New York City. They both claimed it was love at first sight, and they hit it off instantly. Like Depp, Moss had been targeted as the subject of public scrutiny; she was criticized for her waiflike figure, and tabloids hinted that she had an eating disorder. She could easily relate to Depp's experience with being mislabeled. One of the things that attracted Depp most was that Moss shared his dark sense of humor. "She makes me laugh," he says. "And, man, you can't beat that South London accent."[49]

Then their relationship became the subject of tabloid scrutiny after an incident at the Mark Hotel in New York City. One night

Kate Moss

Kate Moss, who dated Johnny Depp for four years in the mid-1990s, is no stranger to controversy. At the prime of her career, she was one of the most successful supermodels, earning up to ten thousand dollars a day. But her waiflike figure and reported health problems sparked rumors of drug abuse and anorexia.

Moss was discovered at JFK Airport in New York City at age fourteen while waiting for a flight home to London. She did her first runway show at age fifteen, and when she was eighteen she became the face of the Calvin Klein ad campaign. This high-profile campaign gained national attention because of Moss's unusually thin figure, and many people speculated that she had an eating disorder. Then, in November 1998, Moss checked into a London clinic to be treated for exhaustion, but many speculated that she was really trying to kick a drug habit. Moss later admitted to heavy drinking and said she had checked into rehab to get sober. Although she and Depp had already split up at that time, he sent her a brand-new BMW as a get-well gift the day she left the clinic. Although she now prefers modeling for fashion magazines to the high-stress job of runway modeling, Moss is still one of the most unique and sought-after supermodels in the industry.

Johnny Depp and supermodel Kate Moss were romantically involved in the early 1990s.

hotel patrons heard loud crashing noises from Depp's room. When hotel staff arrived, they saw that Depp had damaged several pieces of furniture and broken a glass coffee table. Although he offered to pay for the damage, the hotel staff called the police. The next day, the tabloids ran photos of Depp being led away from the hotel in handcuffs, and stories speculated that he had trashed his hotel room after a fight with Moss. Depp insists that he and Moss had not had an argument, but because there seemed to be no reason for his outburst, he gained notoriety for having an out-of-control temper. Even though the hotel declined to press charges against him, Depp found he could not shake the bad-boy image.

Reputation Repair

After the publicity surrounding his run-in at the Mark, Depp wanted to shift the focus back to his acting career. He surprised critics and Hollywood executives by departing from his usual eccentric characters and taking on two leading-man roles, first in *Don Juan de Marco*, then in the thriller *Nick of Time*.

In *Don Juan de Marco*, Depp plays a young man who believes he is the legendary lover Don Juan. Marlon Brando, one of Depp's favorite actors, played his psychiatrist. Although it was unusual for Depp to accept a role as a romantic lead, he was drawn to the character as soon as he read the script. He related to Don Juan's strength and confidence, but also felt that Don Juan's arrogance would be a far stretch from his own personality. He was willing to take on the challenge. Filming the love scenes was awkward; it was something Depp had never become comfortable with, no matter how many times he had to do it. "The atmosphere is too ridiculous," he says. "You're . . . kissing some girl, professing your undying love, and you see that grip over there eating a bologna sandwich."[50] Still, the movie was a modest success, taking in $22 million at the box office.

Depp then took on the lead role in *Nick of Time*. Although Depp was usually known for playing eccentric roles, his character in the movie was a straight-laced businessman. Still, Depp was drawn to the role because his character has to make difficult decisions. He enjoyed playing the conflicted character. Depp also accepted the lead role in the offbeat western *Dead Man*, in which he played a fugitive on the run after murdering a man in self-defense. In portraying these characters, Depp showed that he could successfully tackle extremely diverse roles.

By now Depp had cemented himself as one of the most well-respected actors in Hollywood. Studio executives wanted him to star as a romantic lead, but Depp refused to accept roles that were designed solely for the purpose of making him a superstar, turning down several roles in major blockbusters over the next few years. He passed on the opportunity to play Lestat in *Interview with the Vampire*, and the role ultimately went to Tom Cruise. He also rejected the romantic lead in *Legends of the Fall*, which went to Brad Pitt, and the chance to play an action hero in *Speed*, which proved to be a breakthrough role for Keanu Reeves. Instead, he continued to choose movies that were less commercially appealing but more challenging to him as an actor.

Going Undercover

In 1997 Depp was offered the title role in *Donnie Brasco*, in which Depp played Joe Pistone, an undercover FBI agent who made his way into a New York Mafia family in the 1970s under the false identity of Donnie Brasco. Pistone finds his loyalties tested when a hit

Jim Jarmusch

Independent filmmaker Jim Jarmusch, a friend of Depp's, studied film in New York before making his first film, *Permanent Vacation*, for fifteen thousand dollars. Jarmusch went on to direct several small-budget films that gained critical acclaim at film festivals. Known for his unique approach to storytelling, he created movies that depicted America through the eyes of a foreigner or an outcast, and he often cast unknown actors or musicians in lead roles. When Depp starred in Jarmusch's movie *Dead*

Man, the two friends had the chance to work together on a professional level. "He really is one of the most precise and focused people I've ever worked with," Jarmusch told *Premiere* magazine in February 1995.

Independent filmmaker Jim Jarmusch worked with friend Johnny Depp on Dead Man, *an offbeat Western film.*

man named Lefty takes him under his wing. The two men form a close friendship, but Pistone ultimately testifies against his new mob acquaintances. To this day, there is a five-hundred-thousand-dollar bounty on the real-life Pistone's head.

Depp spent weeks befriending members of the Mafia as research for his role. The movie studio arranged a dinner for Depp, the cast, and a few mobsters. Depp knew that working so closely with the Mafia could be dangerous, especially since he was portraying a mob informant. Still, it was important to him that he understood how the Mafia operated, and he felt that spending time with them helped him to realize the bond between members.

Depp also felt that it was necessary to meet Pistone so he could get a sense of his true personality. Depp did not expect to like him; he assumed Pistone would be arrogant and swaggering. Instead, they got along well. Pistone respected Depp as an actor, and Depp

Depp played undercover Mafia informant Joe Pistone in Donnie Brasco. *The real-life Pistone praised Depp's performance.*

learned to respect Pistone's acting abilities as well. Depp realized that, although he could reshoot a scene several times if he messed up, Pistone had to be perfect every time. Otherwise his Mafia acquaintances would get suspicious, and his life would be in jeopardy. Depp studied Pistone's gestures and habits; he wanted to give Pistone a fair portrayal and show him as an ordinary human being with an out-of-the-ordinary job. Pistone says, "[He] captured me 100 percent—my mannerisms, my walk, my talk. . . . It just comes to him. He's like a sponge."[51]

Although a serious actor, Depp could not suppress his fun-loving side while he was on the set. Once during a scene in a car, he set off a whoopee cushion several times, each time apologizing and blaming the noise on an upset stomach. Finally, just as actor Al Pacino started to get disgusted, Depp revealed his prank. Pacino thought it was so funny that he borrowed the whoopee cushion and tried it out himself.

Depp may have been a prankster, but once the cameras were rolling, he was focused on paying homage to the real-life Pistone. Depp's powerful portrayal in the drama received critical praise, and the movie made more than $40 million at the box office. The action-packed drama also showed that Depp had yet another talent: He could play a convincing action star.

Becoming a Director

Having worked with some of the best directors in Hollywood, Depp was interested in directing a movie himself. After filming wrapped for *Donnie Brasco*, Depp set out to make a movie version of a book called *The Brave*. In the book, Raphael, a poverty-stricken Native American man, is offered a large amount of money to appear in a snuff film, which meant he would actually be killed on screen. Although the character would have to sacrifice his own life, the money would help the character's family survive.

Depp was moved by the man's sacrifice in the book, and he asked his brother, Danny "D.P." Depp, to write the screenplay. He hired extras from a Native American reservation, and invited a Dakota Sioux named Floyd Red Crow Westerman to play Raphael's father. Because of budget constraints, Depp could not afford to hire a lead actor to play Raphael. He would have to star in the movie as well as direct it.

Directing proved to be a far more difficult task than it seemed at first, especially since Depp was also starring in the film. Often he worked a full day on set then spent hours in his trailer making notes for the next day's direction before he began studying his own lines. He did not get to talk to Moss or his family as often as he wanted to, and he begged them to bear with him until he finished shooting the movie.

Depp was also surprised by the amount of responsibility involved in directing. People would ask him such mundane details as what color shoes a character should be wearing in a particular scene. "I thought directing would be easy . . . but it's insane,"[52] he says.

Determined to pay respect to his own Native American heritage, Depp listened to the opinions of the extras on his set and even asked Red Crow to perform a traditional Dakota Sioux sunrise ceremony to bring good luck to the film. Just after he finished, as the sun was coming up, Marlon Brando called to tell Depp he would play the role of McCarthy, the man who is looking to hire Raphael for the snuff film. Depp was certain it was a good omen.

Brando was not the only one of Depp's idols who appeared in the film. Iggy Pop also appeared as a minor character. As it turned out, he did not remember meeting Depp years ago when Depp had insulted him after the concert; when he was reminded, he simply laughed and said it was something he would have done when he was Depp's age. He was happy to work with Depp and respected him for taking on challenging roles and not getting caught up in the glamorous Hollywood lifestyle. "He's out there trying to meet interesting people and challenge himself—as opposed to making constant trips to the hairdresser,"[53] Pop says.

A Crushing Blow

The shoot was demanding, and not merely because of the long hours and overwhelming responsibility. It was being filmed in Death Valley, California, and the cast and crew spent fifty days shooting in the desert in heat that sometimes rose above 120 degrees.

Iggy Pop poses with Depp at the premiere of The Brave *at the 1997 Cannes Film Festival. The film marked Depp's first project as a director.*

Because Depp wanted to premiere the film at the Cannes Film Festival held in Cannes, France, in 1997, he was under a tight time constraint. He had less time than he would have liked to edit the movie, but he was still satisfied with the finished product. At the screening at Cannes, he felt nervous, but he was also proud of the movie. He was relieved when some members of the audience gave him a standing ovation after the movie ended. But while Depp thought the film had been a success, the critics disagreed. "They ate me alive," he says. "I was totally, totally shocked."[54] He did not think the critics had reviewed the movie fairly. Because Depp was often in the tabloid headlines, he felt that some critics had trouble accepting him as a serious movie director. In the end, the film was never released. Nonetheless, Depp was happy with the work he had created. He was so proud of it, in fact, that he had the symbol for *The Brave* tattooed on the inside of his forearm.

Literary Hero

The fate of *The Brave* may have been a letdown for Depp, but soon he had the opportunity to play one of his literary idols. By chance, Depp met one of his favorite authors, Hunter S. Thompson, at a local tavern in Aspen, Colorado, in 1995. Moss had mentioned she wanted to see snow, so Depp took Moss, her mother, and a group of friends to Aspen for a Christmas ski trip. They were sitting in the Woody Creek Tavern, one of Thompson's hangouts, when Thompson burst through the door. Depp was starstruck. He had first read Thompson's semiautobiographical novel *Fear and Loathing in Las Vegas* when he was seventeen, and he was a long-

Depp played one of his literary heroes Hunter S. Thompson in the film version of Thompson's Fear and Loathing in Las Vegas.

time fan. "I was sitting there thinking, 'I'm finally gonna meet Hunter S. Thompson, who I've admired for so many years,'"[55] he says.

The two hit it off, and the group went back to Thompson's house to visit for the evening. Then, while Depp was filming *Donnie Brasco*, Thompson called and told him there might be a movie based on his life, and he thought that Depp would be the perfect actor to portray him. Several months later, an agent called Depp and offered him the lead role in *Fear and Loathing in Las Vegas*.

Becoming Hunter

Depp was thrilled, but first he wanted to make sure Thompson still approved of the idea. Thompson is known for being short-tempered and eccentric; he often dresses in oversized yellow sunglasses and Hawaiian-print shirts, has a history of drug abuse, and collects firearms. Depp worried that Thompson might be offended if he thought Depp's depiction of him was too out-landish or over the top. Depp called him and said, "If I even re-motely do an accurate portrayal, you'll probably hate me for the rest of your life."[56] Nevertheless, Thompson encouraged him to accept the role.

Because Depp deeply admired Thompson's work, it was im-portant that he do a fitting portrayal of him in the movie. As Thompson embarked on a book tour in 1996, Depp joined him to get to know him better. When the book tour stopped in San Francisco, Thompson and Depp spent five days hanging out and discussing all the details of Thompson's life.

After the book tour ended, Depp moved into Thompson's home in Colorado, where he slept in the basement on a small sofa bed surrounded by makeshift bookshelves and lots of spiders. He spent four months analyzing Thompson's mannerisms and learn-ing his subtle habits and gestures. Before he left, Depp allowed Thompson to shave off his signature long locks for the movie. To get into character, Depp drove Thompson's prized Chevrolet convertible, the Red Shark, from Colorado to Los Angeles for the first day of filming. Depp drove with the top down, listening to the same music Thompson had listened to on his original trip to Las Vegas on which the movie was based.

Depp asked Thompson to remain in Colorado while the movie was being filmed. He was nervous and did not want Thompson present on the movie set. "It's hard enough to take that book and translate it into film without having the author of the book around screeching, 'That's not right!'"[57] he says. But Depp would often call Thompson from the set to ask him questions, such as how he would react in a certain situation.

In *Fear and Loathing*, Raoul Duke is a journalist who drives to Las Vegas to cover an off-road motorcycle race. Instead, the excursion turns into a reckless, drug-fueled road trip. The movie was initially criticized for being prodrug, although Depp argued that the film did not promote or encourage drug use in any way. Still, the heavy drug use in the movie did little to quell rumors that Depp was still involved in drugs. Even though he had straightened out his wild lifestyle, his portrayal of Thompson's drug-fueled frenzy was so precise that it was not surprising that some viewers assumed Depp himself was still engaging in the same debauchery as his character in the movie.

Depp's reputation for being a rebel stuck with him, and for a time it seemed as though it would be impossible to overcome. Then a chance meeting changed his life and helped to alter the way people perceived him.

Chapter 5

Finding Happiness

W ITH STANDOUT PERFORMANCES in *Donnie Brasco* and *Fear and Loathing in Las Vegas*, Depp had proven he was one of the most versatile actors in Hollywood. He continued to pursue widely diverse movie roles, but also appeared in several big-budget movies, an unusual occurrence for him. While filming the sci-fi thriller *The Ninth Gate*, he met Vanessa Paradis and ultimately changed the course of his life.

Back-to-Back Disappointments

In early 1998, Depp's relationship with Moss had started to cool off, and they decided to end their four-year romance. After the split, Depp saw reminders of Moss everywhere. She was still one of the world's most popular supermodels, and her photos were plastered on billboards and in magazines all over the country. Rather than being upset by the constant reminders of his ex-girlfriend, though, Depp found that they helped him cope with the breakup. "Seeing [photos of] Kate is comforting," he said at the time. "It eases the pain."[58]

Depp was still reeling from his breakup with Moss when director Roman Polanski asked him to star in the supernatural thriller *The Ninth Gate*. In the movie, Depp plays Dean Corso, a rare-books dealer who is hired by a scholar to find the last remaining copies of a satanic novel called *The Nine Gates of the Kingdom of Shadows*.

Depp traveled to France to film the movie, but almost immediately the on-set atmosphere became tense. Depp and

During filming of The Ninth Gate, *Depp and director Roman Polanski argued constantly over how Depp should play the character of Dean Corso.*

Polanski, both very obstinate and strong minded, each had a clear idea of how Depp should play the character of Corso. Depp respected Polanski's skills as a director and knew he could learn a lot by working with him, but he was frustrated when they could not see eye to eye. Depp and Polanski argued constantly.

Fate Steps In

One night, after a difficult day on set, Depp went to a bar in Paris to unwind. There he spotted French singer-actress Vanessa Paradis. Depp, too nervous to invite her to join him, enlisted a friend to approach her. She accepted his invitation and they spent the rest of the evening together. Within a few weeks, they had started dating.

The Ninth Gate was not terribly successful. But although the shoot was difficult and the movie's reception disappointing, the movie had brought Depp to France. Consequently, Depp believes that meeting Paradis was the real reason he was meant to work on *The Ninth Gate.* He says of their encounter, "It was kind of a strange and beautiful destiny."[59]

Several months after they started dating, Depp and Paradis got exciting news: Paradis was pregnant. Depp was overjoyed that he was going to become a father. He had always wanted to start a family but was not sure that he would meet the right woman—until he found Paradis.

However, Depp had once again found himself in a high-profile romance, and he still could not get used to the constant stream of gossip printed about him in the tabloids. Once he even read a rumor that he had a romantic relationship with Madonna. According to the story, he flew to Miami to visit her and they went swimming

Vanessa Paradis

Depp's longtime girlfriend, Vanessa Paradis, has been a superstar in France since the age of seven when she performed on a televised talent show. Paradis had her first hit single, "Joe Le Taxi," at the age of fourteen and the following year she released her first album. She appeared in her first film when she was seventeen and became the spokeswoman for Coco Chanel perfume at age nineteen.

Stateside, Paradis is best known for her relationship with Depp, but in France she is as popular as Cher or Madonna in the States. She collaborated with singer Lenny Kravitz on her last album, and earned rave reviews for her performance in the movie *La Fille Sur le Pont.* She has proven herself to be a multitalented performer, and in Depp, she has found her equal.

Depp's girlfriend Vanessa Paradis has been a superstar in France since childhood.

in her pool. Depp thought the story was funny since he had never met Madonna.

Although he was able to laugh about his rumored romance, he did not like being followed by the media every time he left his house. One night he and Paradis were leaving a restaurant when paparazzi pounced on them, hoping to get a photo of Depp with his pregnant girlfriend. Depp was annoyed at them for interrupting his romantic evening with Paradis. After he calmly asked the photographers to leave, they moved in, snapping photos. "They were pretty aggressive,"[60] he says. Depp panicked, and in a fit of anger, picked up a piece of wood and threatened the photographers with it. Someone alerted the police and they arrested Depp. He spent several hours in jail, but the photographers declined to press charges.

A New Home

Despite that unpleasant incident, Depp felt he had more privacy in France than he did in Los Angeles. Although the paparazzi were aggressive at times, his French fans respected his privacy. He decided to keep his house in Los Angeles, which had taken seven months to rebuild after it was destroyed in the 1994 earthquake, so he would have somewhere to stay when he traveled there to meet with agents and producers. But he bought another house in the south of France where he could spend most of his time with Paradis, far away from Hollywood. He even opened a restaurant in Paris so he would have somewhere to hang out. Along with fellow actors Sean Penn and John Malkovich, and record producer Thierry Klemeniuk, Depp opened the restaurant Man Ray in 1999. Named for the surrealist painter and photographer, the restaurant quickly became a favorite hangout for fashion designers, actors, and musicians. Depp's newfound appreciation of French culture was apparent in the menu, which included tomato sorbet and roasted frog legs. The Parisian Man Ray was so popular that the owners opened another location in downtown Manhattan in 2001. Like its French predecessor, the club quickly became a popular celebrity haunt, although it closed in 2003.

Depp was having success with all his business ventures. Even the Viper Room, which for a while had been inextricably linked

The success of Depp's Paris restaurant Man Ray prompted him to open a second location in Manhattan (pictured here). Depp has been extremely successful as an entrepreneur.

to River Phoenix's death, was once again best known as a relaxed, trendy club where guests could hang out with friends and listen to live music. Although Phoenix's death was never forgotten, Depp says the club is once again a fun place. He has made it clear that drugs are strictly prohibited in the club. Not all patrons have abided by his rules, though. A few years after Phoenix's death, Depp was in the bathroom of the Viper Room and overheard two patrons in a stall preparing to use cocaine. After the incident with Phoenix, he was outraged that they would think it was acceptable to use drugs in his club. He grabbed the patrons by their collars and had the bouncer throw them out. "That really put me in a hideous rage,"[61] he said. He had worked hard to rebuild his club's reputation, and he did not want to endure another tragedy.

Depp's Favorite Legend

Meanwhile, Depp's career was gaining momentum. After he finished work on *The Ninth Gate*, he was offered a part in a new Tim Burton movie, *Sleepy Hollow*. The movie would be an adaptation of the Washington Irving novel *The Legend of Sleepy Hollow* about a timid detective named Ichabod Crane who is hired to track down a serial killer who is beheading his victims. The people in the village have nicknamed the murderer the Headless Horseman. Depp was familiar with *The Legend of Sleepy Hollow;* when he was growing up, his family would tell the story every Halloween. It was a family tradition and one of Depp's favorite stories, even though as a child the spooky tale terrified him and he would be afraid to walk to the bathroom alone at night because he imagined that the Headless Horseman would be waiting for him.

After the frustration of working on *The Ninth Gate*, Depp was glad to have the chance to work with Burton again: "It's like returning home after a war,"[62] he said. Depp knew that Burton would trust his instincts and give him the freedom to develop his character the way he wanted to.

Although Depp enjoyed filming the movie, there was one aspect of the shoot that did not go smoothly. Crane spends much of the movie on horseback, and the horse, Goldeneye, was defiant and bad tempered. Several times, he tried to bite Depp or throw him off during a scene. Nonetheless, when Depp found out that Goldeneye was going to be euthanized after filming, he decided to keep the horse. He had recently purchased a horse farm in Kentucky for his mother and stepfather, so he had no trouble finding somewhere for Goldeneye to stay.

Working with Ricci

In *Sleepy Hollow*, Crane falls for one of the women in the village, played by actress Christina Ricci. Depp and Ricci first met on the set of *Mermaids*, a drama Ricci had been filming with Winona Ryder while Ryder and Depp were dating. At the time, Ricci was only eight years old, and Depp thought of her as a little sister. Even though in *Sleepy Hollow*, most of the emotion was conveyed through facial expressions rather than through passionate kissing scenes, Depp found it difficult to film romantic scenes with Ricci. "That was a little odd at first,"[63] he says.

Still, he admired Ricci as an actress and was glad to have the chance to work with her. Like Depp, she often chose interesting movies over guaranteed blockbusters. Ricci was also a big fan of Depp's. "He's just really genuine," she says. "He's also an amazing actor, and look at him—he's beautiful."[64]

Of course, the tabloids told a different story. They reported that Depp and Ricci were having a wild fling while Paradis was at home pregnant with Depp's child. The magazines reported that Depp and Ricci had been spotted kissing in a pub in London. Ricci refuted the rumors, saying that she and Depp were like brother and sister.

A Spooky Success

Depp wanted his character to look like Crane as he had been described in Irving's novel. According to the original story, Crane was tall and thin with a long nose and large ears. Depp hoped that the on-set makeup artists would give him a prosthetic nose and ears and was disappointed when studio executives rejected that idea. They did not want Depp's subtle facial expressions to get lost behind layers of makeup, and they also realized that making Depp unattractive was not the best way to draw an audience.

Because Depp thought of Christina Ricci as a little sister, he felt uncomfortable filming the romantic scenes of Sleepy Hollow *with her.*

Although Depp did not get to re-create Crane's physical oddities, Burton encouraged him to capture Crane's eccentric personality. Depp portrayed Crane as a squeamish, easily frightened detective. In one scene, Crane explores a cave in search of the Headless Horseman, and pushes one of the children from town into the cave ahead of him as a shield. Depp's interpretation of Crane as a jittery detective brought comic relief to the film, and it was a major commercial success. It brought in $30 million in its opening weekend, and eventually grossed more than $100 million at the box office. It was, by far, Depp's biggest hit yet.

A New Life

With so many movie roles on his résumé, Depp was eagerly anticipating the opportunity to play the one role he had been wait-

Depp became a father in the spring of 1999 when Paradis gave birth to a baby girl.

ing for: father. On May 27, 1999, Paradis gave birth to a baby girl.
Because they could not decide between the names Lily and Rose,
Depp and Paradis named her Lily-Rose Melody Depp. Depp es-
pecially liked it because it reminded him of his mother's name,
Betty Sue. Both Depp and Paradis love music, so Melody was a
natural choice for their daughter's middle name.

While Paradis was giving birth, paparazzi lined up outside the
couple's hotel waiting to get a glimpse of the new parents when
they returned. Once Lily-Rose was ready to leave the hospital,
Depp and Paradis had to sneak out through the parking garage to
avoid photographers. When they arrived at their house, they were
shocked to see a helicopter hovering over their home, hoping to
snap a photo of the couple and their baby. He and Paradis waited
in the car until the photographers in the helicopter finally gave
up and left.

Depp still disliked the media attention, but he could not have
been happier with his new family. "[Vanessa] is the most beautiful woman in the world . . . and my daughter is the most beautiful creature ever invented,"[65] he gushed. He said becoming a father helped him put his life in perspective and made him
understand why he was alive. "Suddenly you realize, 'Ah, that's
what it's for,'"[66] he says.

Happily taking on the role of a proud father, Depp helped
Paradis with diaper duty and took his newborn daughter for
stroller rides around town. Sometimes he took her to the village
store or brought her along when he went for a cup of coffee. He
enjoyed the privacy of his house in the country, and loved spending time with his family. "I'm just another dad with his daughter,"[67] he says.

The birth of Lily-Rose inspired Depp to give up his self-
destructive habits. Depp declared that his reckless lifestyle was
behind him, and he had learned to center his life around his daughter. "I don't want to poison myself anymore," he says. "Vanessa
and the baby have really given me a reason to live."[68] The for-
merly depressed, brooding Depp was now a doting father and
shared his happiness with anyone who asked. "This baby has given
me life," he says. "I see this amazing, beautiful, pure angel thing
wake up in the morning and smile, and nothing can touch that."[69]

Depp's Homeland

When Depp moved to France, he wanted to be as close to Paradis and as far from Hollywood as possible. Despite his run-in with the paparazzi in 1999, he maintains that he has far more privacy in France than he did while living in Los Angeles. He also worried about raising his daughter in Los Angeles, and felt she would be safer in the French countryside.

Depp's decision to leave the United States caused controversy after a German newspaper reported that Depp had criticized America. According to a *CNN Crossfire* report in 2003, Depp had said, "[America] is something like a dumb puppy that has big teeth that can bite and hurt you." Depp argues that the quote was taken out of context; he had meant that America was a new country compared to England and France, and was still growing as a nation. He immediately apologized for the misquote and told the Scottish newspaper the *Sunday Herald*, "I'm American and I love my country."

Playing a Romantic Lead

Depp did not want to spend a single day away from his girlfriend and daughter, so he was excited to be offered a role in director Lasse Halstrom's romantic drama *Chocolat* set in Europe. This meant Depp did not have to travel far from his home or his family to film it. "It is really hard to leave home when you're surrounded by all that beauty,"[70] he says.

When Halstrom made it clear that he did not want to take no for an answer, Depp was taken aback by his insistence. On the set of Halstrom's movie *What's Eating Gilbert Grape*, Depp had been depressed and difficult to work with, so he figured Halstrom would be reluctant to work with him again. "I was surprised," he says. "But I was so happy to work with him again, to redeem myself."[71] He gladly accepted the role, and was thrilled to work alongside Juliette Binoche and highly regarded actress Judi Dench. Although Depp had sworn he never wanted to play a romantic lead, the beautifully written movie was enough to attract his interest. *Chocolat* was a lighthearted romance, which matched Depp's state of mind at that time.

Filming the movie had one odd side effect: It made Depp despise chocolate. In the movie, Depp's character falls in love with a woman who owns a chocolate shop. The chocolate used in the film was rich and dark, and Halstrom shot so many takes of Depp eating it that Depp could barely even look at the candy after filming was finished.

    Chocolat received widespread critical recognition and was nominated for several Academy Awards, including Best Picture and Best Adapted Screenplay. Although Depp was not nominated,

Depp becomes the first person to walk on his star on Hollywood's Walk of Fame in 1999. In that year Depp starred in the critically acclaimed Chocolat.

that year he received recognition of his own; he was awarded a star on the Hollywood Walk of Fame. Depp was also given an honorary Cesar, the French equivalent of an Oscar, for his lifetime achievement as an actor. Depp was slightly troubled by that award, because he knew that he was nowhere near finished with his acting career.

Continued Success

Following the success of *Chocolat,* Depp played a cross-dressing lieutenant in *Before Night Falls,* a film about Cuban poet Reinaldo Arenas who joined dictator Fidel Castro's band of rebels in 1959 during the Cuban revolution before eventually leaving Cuba for New York City. Again, the role required Depp to wear lipstick and high heels on the set; luckily he had plenty of practice on the set of *Ed Wood.*

Then, in the drama *The Man Who Cried,* Depp plays a Gypsy horseman named Cesar who falls in love with a Jewish émigré from Russia. When she learns of the Nazis' plans to invade Paris and round up Jews and Gypsies, she wants to stay and fight, but Cesar encourages her to leave for America. Once again, Ricci was playing Depp's love interest, but this time they had to film risqué love scenes. Although it was uncomfortable at first, eventually both actors learned to find humor in filming such awkward scenes.

The role required other preparations as well. Depp had to have gold teeth bonded onto his own. It was not a pleasant process. The gold caps were permanently bonded onto his teeth, so after filming, he had to get the caps chipped off by a dentist.

To study for the role, Depp spent time with a band of Romanian Gypsies. He says the Gypsies told him to appreciate everything in his life, not just material possessions or career accomplishments. "Those guys appreciate . . . every moment, every breath they take,"[72] he says.

It seemed as though Depp was taking that advice to heart. With his new family he had found the secret to happiness. Depp began to approach his career with a fresh perspective and an uncharacteristically optimistic outlook.

Chapter 6

Back on Top

WITH HIS TROUBLEMAKER reputation behind him, Depp was able to focus once again on his acting. Though he continued to take on unique and eccentric roles, a series of successful major films proved Depp's commercial appeal.

A Familiar Role

When Depp was given the chance to star in *Blow*, he readily accepted. In the biopic, Depp portrays real-life drug smuggler George Jung. Frustrated with his financially unstable father and overly critical mother, Jung decides to find success any way he can. He starts dealing drugs, and his small "business" soon expands into a national drug-smuggling ring. Jung eventually travels to Colombia to increase his supply and ends up becoming the biggest drug trafficker in the United States. Soon, however, his dangerous occupation catches up to him, and he is arrested and sentenced to sixty years in prison.

Depp knew that he might have easily suffered the same fate. He, too, watched as his blue-collar parents sometimes struggled to provide for their family, and, like Jung, he had turned to drugs when his difficult home life had become too much to bear. But Depp had found music as an outlet for his frustration.

Depp felt he had an understanding of Jung's character, and he liked that the movie was a cautionary tale without being preachy. Still, Depp wanted to make sure he liked and respected Jung as a person before he could bring his character to life in a movie. Director Ted Demme encouraged Depp to read Jung's

Depp's portrayal of drug kingpin George Jung in Blow *was so convincing that it moved the real Jung to tears.*

autobiography and meet him at the prison where he was serving his sentence.

Depp spent two days visiting Jung at Otisville Penitentiary in Otisville, New York, asking him questions about his life and studying the way he talked and acted. Each time he visited, he had to walk through metal detectors and empty his pockets, and he had to go through a series of high-security metal doors to reach Jung. It was an unsettling environment for Depp.

It was important to Depp that he get to know Jung as a person, not just as a notorious criminal. He wanted to understand why Jung made the choices he made so he could have a better appreciation of the character he was playing. He was saddened when he listened to stories about Jung's family. While Depp had been fortunate enough to find happiness with Paradis and Lily-Rose, Jung had been torn away from his wife and children when he was imprisoned.

After meeting with Jung, Depp felt that he had a grasp on Jung's mannerisms and the way he would react in certain situations. Demme trusted Depp's instincts so much that he allowed

Depp to improvise much of his dialogue throughout the film. Depp's commitment to capturing Jung's story paid off. Jung was so moved by Depp's portrayal of his life that he reportedly cried through the final half hour of the movie. *Blow* was a box-office success, taking in more than $52 million.

Back in the Limelight

After the success of *Blow*, Depp was offered a starring role in *From Hell*, a grisly thriller based on the real-life story of Jack the Ripper. Depp plays Fred Abberline, an inspector who is obsessed with finding the serial killer who terrorized England by murdering several London prostitutes in the late 1800s.

Depp had been intrigued with the story of Jack the Ripper for many years. When he was seven years old, he had watched a documentary on the case and was fascinated by the fact that such a horrific crime had gone unsolved for more than a century. Depp did not have to do much research for the movie, because he was already so educated on the topic. He was excited to have the chance to explore the story that had mesmerized him so much as a child. "It was just such a golden opportunity,"[73] he says.

Depp was back in the spotlight, and audiences were once again drawn to his inimitable talent for playing unique and challenging characters. Whether Depp liked it or not, they also took notice of his striking good looks, and in 2001, Depp was voted one of *People* magazine's "50 Most Beautiful People in the World." Although Depp preferred to be recognized for his skills as an actor, many respected directors who had worked with him commented on Depp's good looks in the magazine. "Johnny's cheekbones are insane,"[74] remarked Ted Demme, who added that female crew members would line up around the monitors on set when Depp was filming close-up scenes. Each time he called "cut," he would hear a collective sigh from the crew members.

Depp, not wanting to be thought of as a pretty face, rebelled against that image. He continued to dress in his signature ripped jeans and ratty T-shirts, with his long hair falling in his face. He was so unconcerned with fashion that he hardly owned any dress clothes. One night before attending a formal dinner party in Paris, Depp realized he did not have an appropriate dress shirt to wear.

He went to Man Ray and asked one of his waiters to lend him the shirt he was wearing. As a thank-you, he offered the waiter one hundred dollars before heading out to the fancy dinner.

A Movie Unmade

While Depp was working on *From Hell*, Burton approached him about another movie he was working on, a remake of the 1968 classic *Planet of the Apes*. Although Depp would have loved to work with Burton again, he turned down the opportunity. He had already agreed to work on a movie called *The Man Who Killed Don Quixote*, in which Depp would play an advertising executive who travels back in time and becomes Quixote's sidekick, Sancho Panza. Depp did not want to pass up the role. He loved the story of Don Quixote, and he was anxious to work again with director Terry Gilliam, who Depp befriended after Gilliam directed *Fear and Loathing in Las Vegas*. He was also going to get the chance to work alongside Paradis, who had been cast as his love interest, Lady Dulcinea.

At first, the *Don Quixote* shoot went smoothly, but suddenly everything seemed to go wrong. Flash floods destroyed part of the set, and Jean Rausberg, the actor who was playing Quixote, reportedly suffered a back injury. Because the part of Quixote required Rausberg to ride a horse throughout much of the filming, shooting was halted while the actor recovered. The movie was being filmed on a tight budget, and they could not afford the delays in shooting and the damage to the set. After six days, the project was canceled. "It was a disastrous relief,"[75] Depp says.

A New Addition

In June 2002, Depp and Paradis welcomed another child, a son they named Jack. While Lily-Rose was the princess of the family, Jack had a different role. "My boy is like this . . . warrior,"[76] Depp bragged. He was perfectly content to stay at home with his girlfriend and their children, playing Barbies with Lily-Rose and watching Jack learn to walk and talk. Being a father brought him a happiness he never dreamed he could achieve. "I want 100 more children,"[77] he says.

Don Quixote: What Went Wrong?

Depp's role in *The Man Who Killed Don Quixote* eventually evolved into an unanticipated role in *Lost in La Mancha*, a documentary of the collapse of the ill-fated movie. For decades, director Terry Gilliam wanted to make a movie adaptation of the seventeenth-century novel *Don Quixote*, about a slightly unbalanced man on who sets out on horseback in search of adventure and romance. The film was made on a tight budget, but problems arose almost immediately. Fighter jets flew over the set, interfering with filming by creating sonic booms. A storm flooded the set and damaged camera equipment. The lead actor injured his back and could not work; if they waited for him to recover, several of the other actors would have to drop out of the movie because of scheduling conflicts. Eventually the movie was cancelled.

Director Terry Gilliam and Depp discuss a scene during filming of the abandoned project The Man Who Killed Don Quixote.

Depp stayed true to his promise to give up his bad-boy antics. Once he became enraged when a magazine printed a photo of Lily-Rose. While he understood that he and Paradis would be subject to constant media attention, he did not think it was fair for the media to use Lily-Rose's photo, thus violating her privacy. His initial instinct was to attack the reporter who had printed the photo. Instead, he controlled his temper, met with the reporter, and calmly explained why he thought it was unethical to print a photo of his daughter.

Pirate Treasure

Soon after his son was born, Depp accepted a risky role in the adventure movie *Pirates of the Caribbean: The Curse of the Black Pearl*. Depp was cast as pirate captain Jack Sparrow who sets out to stop a band of evil pirates from stealing a precious medallion. The film was a risky venture: Another pirate movie, *Cutthroat Island*, had come out several years before and lost nearly $90 million. It seemed to indicate that there was no real market for pirate movies. Producers were undeterred, though, and spent approximately $135 million creating *Pirates of the Caribbean*.

Depp was not concerned about whether the movie was a potential hit. To him, the role was an opportunity of a lifetime. As a child, he listened over and over to the story of Blackbeard the pirate. When he got the script, Depp said, "I felt nine years old again."[78]

Once again, Depp put all his energy into becoming his character—this time Jack Sparrow. He was so convincing that he even confused his own daughter. Although Lily-Rose understood that her mother was a singer and actress, she believed that Depp was actually a pirate.

Depp admits to a lifelong fascination with pirates, and he eagerly accepted the role of Jack Sparrow in the blockbuster film Pirates of the Caribbean.

At times Depp and the producers clashed when it came to their ideas of how the character of Sparrow should be played. For example, Depp wanted his character to have gold teeth, but producers thought that Depp should be as attractive as possible in order to attract audiences. Depp did not want Sparrow to be a sexy, swashbuckling pirate, so he asked his dentist to put gold caps on a few extra teeth. That way, when producers inevitably complained, he would be able to bargain and keep at least a few of the gold teeth. "I just had to say, 'Listen, trust me or fire me. . . . Once everything's all put together, I think you'll like it.'"[79] In the end, Sparrow had several gold teeth, along with beads, braids, and coins tied into his unkempt hair.

Depp ended up staying in character longer than he had anticipated. After filming wrapped, he was so excited to return home and see his family that he hopped the first plane to Paris. Halfway there, he remembered that he still had his gold teeth—and the dentist who could remove the caps was now five thousand miles away in Los Angeles.

Depp's instincts on how to play the character of Sparrow proved to be right. The movie earned more than $70 million during its first five days in theaters and ultimately grossed more than $650 million worldwide. It was by far Depp's most commercially successful film and proved that he could play an unkempt, offbeat character and still attract a large mainstream audience. "It was awesome to watch Johnny," says his costar, Orlando Bloom. "He always creates a character that is so different."[80] Though it was rare for Depp to do a summer blockbuster, he loved the script, and says he would happily do a sequel if he was asked. "It would be nice to have a hugely successful film . . . especially one that you did because you loved doing it."[81]

A Bright Future

Depp followed up *Pirates* with another smash hit, *Once Upon a Time in Mexico*. In the action adventure, Depp plays a rogue CIA agent who recruits a reclusive hero to help him foil a plot to assassinate the president of Mexico. The film brought in more than $43 million at the box office. Although Depp had once again chosen the role for its unique characters and interesting story line, lately it seemed that his choices were striking a chord with mainstream audiences.

Looking back at his past roles, Depp says he never tried to shun mainstream movies. He simply chose characters he could connect with, regardless of the film's commercial potential. "My job is to do things I believe in, to play parts that give me the opportunity to bring something interesting," he says. "I have nothing against the idea of taking part in a big-budget movie if the story is good."[82]

By 2003, he had plenty of varied projects lined up for the future. In the thriller *Secret Window*, Depp will play Mort, a writer who is stalked by a strange man who accuses him of plagiarizing his work. He will also star in an adaptation of another of Thompson's novels, *The Rum Diary*, in which he will play a man involved in a tangled romance in Puerto Rico. He is slated to play *Peter Pan* author James Barrie in the upcoming film *Neverland*, and is cast in the lead role, Willy Wonka, in a remake of *Charlie and the Chocolate Factory*, which Burton will be directing.

Family Man

Depp has become a hot commodity once again, but the fame no longer bothers him like it used to. Now he knows he can turn to his family whenever he needs a break from the spotlight. He makes time to visit his mom in Southern California, and he spends as much time with Paradis, Lily-Rose, and Jack as he possibly can. Since Lily-Rose was born, the most time he has spent away from home continuously was seventeen days—and even that was difficult for him to endure.

Depp knows his days as a struggling rock star are over, but he still makes music a part of his life. In 2000, he helped Paradis work on her new album titled *Bliss*. "I don't think of music as a novelty," Depp says. "It's still my first love—absolutely. Music is a real sensual thing. You can hear a song and it takes you right back to that moment . . . whenever you first heard it."[83]

As of 2003 Depp and Paradis were still not engaged; they would prefer to wait until their children are grown before they plan a wedding so the whole family can be involved in the celebration. Neither Depp nor Paradis worries about marriage at the

Today Johnny Depp is a devoted family man and one of the most sought-after actors in Hollywood.

moment; they are happy just being together. "We are just like one person," Paradis says. "I've never met a personality as beautiful as his."[84] Depp feels the same way about her. "I've been blessed with an amazing relationship with an amazing girl,"[85] he says.

Endless Possibilities

As for his career, Depp is still amazed at his success. Many years ago, he promised himself he would never choose a role just to make money, and he has stayed true to his word. "Every film I've done, I'm happy I made that choice," he says. "I don't have any regrets whatsoever."[86] He has earned respect from his peers, even if he is still a prankster who enjoys checking into hotels under pseudonyms like Mr. Stench.

Depp has become one of the most sought-after actors in Hollywood. He never hesitates to take risks and directors rely on him to bring life to challenging and complicated characters. Even in unconventional roles, he attracts a mainstream audience to theaters. His mother is amazed by what he has accomplished in his career. "Sometimes she still looks at me and says, 'Can you believe your life?'"[87] Depp says. After all, Johnny Depp has demonstrated his merit as a genuine star, and he has barely begun to show audiences what he is capable of.

Notes

Chapter 1: Wild Child

1. Quoted in Kevin Cook, "Johnny Depp," *Playboy*, January 1996, p. 49.
2. Quoted in Kevin Sessums, "Johnny Be Good," *Vanity Fair*, February 1997. www.johnnydeppfan.com.
3. Quoted in Cook, "Johnny Depp," p. 49.
4. Quoted in Cook, "Johnny Depp," p. 49.
5. Quoted in Elizabeth McCracken, "Depp Charge," *Elle*, June 1998. www.johnnydeppfan.com.
6. Quoted in Karen Hardy Bystedt, *Before They Were Famous*. Santa Monica: General Publishing Group, 1996. www.johnnydeppfan.com.
7. Quoted in Steve Pond, "Depp Perception," *US*, June 26, 1989. www.johnnydeppfan.com.
8. Quoted in Elaine Warren, "Bad Boy to Role Model," *TV Guide*, January 23, 1988. www.johnnydeppfan.com.
9. Quoted in Cindy Pearlman, "Here's Johnny!" *Model*, December 1988. www.johnnydeppfan.com.
10. Quoted in James Ryan, "Depp Gets Deeper," *Vogue*, September 1994. www.johnnydeppfan.com.
11. Quoted in Tom Shone, "Johnny Depp Isn't Johnny Depp Anymore," *Talk*, October 1999. www.johnnydeppfan.com.
12. Quoted in Cook, "Johnny Depp," p. 49.
13. Quoted in Cook, "Johnny Depp," p. 49.
14. Quoted in Johnny Deppfan.com, "Transcript: *Inside the Actor's Studio*," September 8, 2002. www.johnnydeppfan.com.
15. Quoted in Dagmar Dunlevy, "Johnny Depp," *Flare*, November 2001. www.johnnydeppfan.com.

16. Quoted in Johnny Deppfan.com, "Transcript: *Inside the Actor's Studio*."

17. Quoted in Johnny Deppfan.com, "Transcript: *Inside the Actor's Studio*."

18. Quoted in John Waters, "Johnny Depp," *Interview*, April 1990. www.johnnydeppfan.com.

Chapter 2: A Change in Plans

19. Quoted in Pond, "Depp Perception."

20. Quoted in Stephen Rebello, "Johnny Handsome," *Movieline*, May 1990. www.johnnydeppfan.com.

21. Quoted in Chris Heath, "Portrait of the Oddest as a Young Man," *Details*, May 1993. www.johnnydeppfan.com.

22. Quoted in Pond, "Depp Perception."

23. Quoted in Jamie Diamond, "Johnny Depp," *Cosmopolitan*, 1993. www.johnnydeppfan.com.

24. Quoted in Warren, "Bad Boy to Role Model."

25. Quoted in Warren, "Bad Boy to Role Model."

26. Quoted in Pearlman, "Here's Johnny!"

27. Quoted in Johnny Deppfan.com, "Transcript: *The Charlie Rose Show*," November 15, 1999. www.johnnydeppfan.com.

28. Quoted in Diamond, "Johnny Depp."

Chapter 3: Finding His Niche

29. Quoted in Heath, "Portrait of the Oddest as a Young Man."

30. Quoted in Christina Kelly, "Johnny Depp from A to W," *Sassy*, May 1990. www.johnnydeppfan.com.

31. Quoted in Waters, "Johnny Depp."

32. Quoted in Stephen Rebello, "Johnny Depp Lets Down His Hair," *Movieline*, April 1993. www.johnnydeppfan.com.

33. Quoted in Chris Willman, "From Baby Face to 'Cry-Baby,'" *Los Angeles Times*, April 4, 1990, p. F1.

34. Quoted in William Georgiades, "An American in Paris," *Detour*, December 1999/January 2000. www.johnnydeppfan.com.

35. Quoted in Rebello, "Johnny Handsome."

36. Quoted in Johnny Deppfan.com, "Transcript: *The Charlie Rose Show*."

37. Quoted in Johnny Deppfan.com, "Transcript: *Inside the Actor's Studio.*"

38. Quoted in Rebello, "Johnny Depp Lets Down His Hair."

39. Quoted in Dana Shapiro, "What Makes Johnny Famous?" *Icon*, June 1998. www.johnnydeppfan.com.

40. Quoted in Steve Goldman, "Depp Water," *Empire*, June 1997. www.johnnydeppfan.com.

41. Quoted in Shapiro, "What Makes Johnny Famous?"

42. Quoted in Bruce Kirkland, "From Punk to Passion," *Toronto Sun*, March 19, 1995, p. S3.

43. Quoted in Hilary de Vries, "The Normalization of Johnny Depp," *Los Angeles Times*, December 12, 1993, p. 3.

Chapter 4: Hard Times

44. Quoted in Lucy Kaylin, "Johnny in Paradise," *GQ*, August 2003. p. 96.

45. Quoted in de Vries, "The Normalization of Johnny Depp."

46. Quoted in Ryan, "Depp Gets Deeper."

47. Quoted in William Keck, "A Window into His Soul," *Los Angeles Times*, April 1, 2001. www.johnnydeppfan.com.

48. Quoted in Holly Millea, "Ghost in the Machine," *Premiere*, February 1995. www.johnnydeppfan.com.

49. Quoted in Sessums, "Johnny Be Good."

50. Quoted in Cook, "Johnny Depp," p. 49.

51. Quoted in Richard Schickel, "Depp Charge," *Time*, March 3, 1997, p. 70.

52. Quoted in Natasha Stoynoff, "Bleeding Hearts," *Toronto Sun*, February 23, 1997, p. S18.

53. Quoted in Thomas Beller, "Fame Is a Four-Letter Word," *Bazaar*, December 1995. www.johnnydeppfan.com.

54. Quoted in Jessamy Calkin, "Johnny Depp Esq.," *Esquire* (UK), February 2000. www.johnnydeppfan.com.

55. Quoted in Jenny Peters, "Narcotics Synonymous," *GQ* (Australia), June 1998. www.johnnydeppfan.com.

56. Quoted in Chris Heath, "Johnny Depp's Savage Journey," *Rolling Stone*, June 11, 1998. www.johnnydeppfan.com.

57. Quoted in Heath, "Johnny Depp's Savage Journey."

Chapter 5: Finding Happiness

58. Quoted in Louis B. Hobson, "Depp of Emotion," *Calgary Sun*, May 17, 1998, p. SE03.
59. Quoted in Tiffany Rose, "Hidden Deppths," *Cosmopolitan* (UK), June 2001. www.johnnydeppfan.com.
60. Quoted in Johnny Deppfan.com, "Transcript: *The Late Show With David Letterman*," November 1999. www.johnnydeppfan.com.
61. Quoted in Keck, "A Window into His Soul."
62. Quoted in Neal Watson, "Depp Charge," *Edmonton Sun*, November 14, 1999, p. SE14.
63. Quoted in Simon Braund, "Village of the Damned," *Empire*, January 2000. www.johnnydeppfan.com.
64. Quoted in Braund, "Village of the Damned."
65. Quoted in Georgiades, "An American in Paris."
66. Quoted in Shone, "Johnny Depp Isn't Johnny Depp Anymore."
67. Quoted in Tiscali Entertainment, "Depp Deals Hollywood a Blow." www.tiscali.co.uk.
68. Quoted in Calkin, "Johnny Depp Esq."
69. Quoted in Johanna Schneller, "Where's Johnny?" *Premiere*, December 1999. www.johnnydeppfan.com.
70. Quoted in Michele Fontanelli, "Blown Away by Whitey," Johnny Depp the Unofficial Site. www.johnyd3pp.20m.com.
71. Quoted in Martha Frankel, "A Man Apart," *Movieline*, March 2001. www.johnnydeppfan.com.
72. Quoted in Johnny Deppfan.com, "Transcript: *Inside the Actor's Studio*."

Chapter 6: Back on Top

73. Quoted in J. Sperling Reich, "Johnny Come Blow Your Horn," Reel.com. www.reel.com.
74. Quoted in *People*, "The 50 Most Beautiful People in the World," May 14, 2001, p. 98.
75. Quoted in Bond, "The Depth of Depp."
76. Quoted in Johnny Deppfan.com, "Transcript: *The Tonight Show with Jay Leno*," June 27, 2003. www.johnnydeppfan.com.
77. Quoted in Louis B. Hobson, "Finally Fulfilled," *Calgary Sun*, April 1, 2001, p. 49.

78. Quoted in Johnny Deppfan.com, "Thrill Ride," *Empire*, September 2003. www.johnnydeppfan.com.

79. Quoted in Kaylin, "Johnny in Paradise."

80. Quoted in Johnny Deppfan.com, "Thrill Ride."

81. Quoted in Johnny Deppfan.com, "Satisfied Mind," *FilmInk*, September 2003. www.johnnydeppfan.com.

82. Quoted in Jacques-André Bondy, "Johnny Goes to Cannes," *Premiere* (France), June 1998. johnnydeppfan.com.

83. Quoted in Brendan Leman, "Johnny Depp," *Interview*, December 1995. www.johnnydeppfan.com.

84. Quoted in Louise Finlay, "Johnny Depp in Paradise," *Elle* (France), January 2000. www.johnnydeppfan.com.

85. Quoted in Rose, "Hidden Deppths."

86. Quoted in Johnny Deppfan.com, "Transcript: *The Charlie Rose Show*."

87. Quoted in Cook, "Johnny Depp," p. 49.

Important Dates in the Life of Johnny Depp

1963

Born June 9 to Betty Sue and John Christopher Depp in Owensboro, Kentucky.

1975

Buys his first electric guitar.

1983

Moves to Los Angeles with his band, The Kids, to pursue a recording contract. Marries makeup artist Lori Allison.

1984

Makes his film debut in *Nightmare on Elm Street;* The Kids disband.

1985

Depp and Allison divorce.

1986

Earns a small role in the Academy Award–winning drama *Platoon*.

1987

Accepts the role of Tom Hanson on *21 Jump Street*.

1989

Begins dating actress Winona Ryder.

1990

Earns breakthrough roles in *Cry-Baby* and *Edward Scissorhands;* leaves *21 Jump Street*.

1993

Stars in *Benny & Joon;* opens the Viper Club in West Hollywood.

1994

Dates actress Kate Moss; arrested after trashing a hotel room in New York; appears in *What's Eating Gilbert Grape* and *Ed Wood*.

1995

Films *Don Juan de Marco, Dead Man,* and *Nick of Time*.

1997

Depp and Moss separate; Depp stars in *Donnie Brasco,* and cowrites, directs, and stars in *The Brave*.

1998

Meets and begins dating Vanessa Paradis; appears in *The Ninth Gate* and *Fear and Loathing in Las Vegas*.

1999

Stars in *Sleepy Hollow;* arrested after threatening paparazzi in London; daughter Lily-Rose Melody Depp is born on May 27.

2000

Appears in *Chocolat*.

2001

Appears in *Blow* and *From Hell*.

2002

Son Jack is born April 9.

2003

Stars in *Pirates of the Caribbean;* appears in *Once Upon a Time in Mexico*.

2004

Wins Screen Actors Guild award for Outstanding Performance by a Male Actor in a Leading Role, and nominated for an Academy Award for Best Actor in a Leading Role for *Pirates of the Caribbean: The Curse of the Black Pearl*.

For Further Reading

Books

Holly George-Warren, *The Rolling Stone Book of the Beats*. New York: Hyperion, 1999. This anthology of essays, photos, and drawings on Beat literature includes an entry by Johnny Depp.

Brian J. Robb, *Johnny Depp: A Modern Rebel*. London: Plexus, 1996. This book explores the highs and lows of Depp's career, from his greatest successes to his most infamous scandals.

Mark Salisbury, *Burton on Burton*. New York: Faber and Faber, 2000. This complete biography of the life and career of acclaimed director Tim Burton includes a foreword by Johnny Depp.

Web Sites

Depp Town (www.depptown.com). This fan site features news and information, a filmography, and a large photo gallery.

E! Online (www.eonline.com). Type his name into the search box for information, articles, and photos.

Johnny Deppfan.com (www.johnnydeppfan.com). This comprehensive Johnny Depp fan site contains an extensive archive of interviews, articles, and transcripts of television appearances.

Yahoo! Movies (www.movies.yahoo.com). A complete list of Depp's past, current, and upcoming film projects.

Works Consulted

Periodicals

Kevin Cook, "Johnny Depp," *Playboy*, January 1996.

Hilary de Vries, "The Normalization of Johnny Depp," *Los Angeles Times*, December 12, 1993.

Louis B. Hobson, "Depp of Emotion," *Calgary Sun*, May 17, 1998.

———, "Finally Fulfilled," *Calgary Sun*, April 1, 2001.

Lucy Kaylin, "Johnny in Paradise," *GQ*, August 2003.

Bruce Kirkland, "Depp Takes It to the Extreme," *Toronto Sun*, May 17, 1998.

———, "From Punk to Passion," *Toronto Sun*, March 19, 1995.

People, "The 50 Most Beautiful People in the World," May 14, 2001.

Peter Ross, "Mast Action Hero" *Sunday Herald,* July 27, 2003.

Richard Schickel, "Depp Charge," *Time*, March 3, 1997.

Natasha Stoynoff, "Bleeding Hearts," *Toronto Sun*, February 23, 1997.

Neal Watson, "Depp Charge," *Edmonton Sun*, November 14, 1999.

Chris Willman, "From Baby Face to 'Cry-Baby,'" *Los Angeles Times*, April 4, 1990.

Internet Sources

Thomas Beller, "Fame Is a Four-Letter Word," *Bazaar*, December 1995. www.johnnydeppfan.com.

Jeff Bond, "The Depth of Depp," Johnny Depp the Unofficial Site. www.johnyd3pp.20m.com.

Jacques-André Bondy, "Johnny Goes to Cannes," *Premiere* (France), June 1998. www.johnnydeppfan.com.

Simon Braund, "Village of the Damned," *Empire,* January 2000. www.johnnydeppfan.com.

Karen Hardy Bystedt, "Before They Were Famous," December 1987. www.johnnydeppfan.com.

Jessamy Calkin, "Johnny Depp Esq.," *Esquire* (UK), February 2000. www.johnnydeppfan.com.

Tucker Carlson and Paul Begala, "Hollywood and Politics." *CNN Crossfire,* October 30, 2003. www.nexis.com.

Jamie Diamond, "Johnny Depp," *Cosmopolitan,* 1993. www.johnny deppfan.com.

Dagmar Dunlevy, "Johnny Depp," *Flare,* November 2001. www.johnnydeppfan.com.

Louise Finlay, "Johnny Depp in Paradise," *Elle* (France), January 2000. www.johnnydeppfan.com.

Michele Fontanelli, "Blown Away by Whitey," Johnny Depp the Unofficial Site. www.johnyd3pp.20m.com.

Martha Frankel, "A Man Apart," *Movieline,* March 2001. www.johnny deppfan.com.

William Georgiades, "An American in Paris," *Detour,* December 1999/January 2000. www.johnnydeppfan.com.

Steve Goldman, "Depp Water," *Empire,* June 1997. www.johnny deppfan.com.

Chris Heath, "Johnny Depp's Savage Journey," *Rolling Stone,* June 11, 1998. www.johnnydeppfan.com.

———, "Portrait of the Oddest as a Young Man," *Details,* May 1993. www.johnnydeppfan.com.

Internet Movie Database, "Johnny Depp." www.imdb.com.

Johnny Deppfan.com, "Satisfied Mind," *FilmInk,* September 2003. www.johnnydeppfan.com.

———, "Thrill Ride," *Empire,* September 2003.

———, "Transcript: *Inside the Actor's Studio,*" September 8, 2002.

———, "Transcript: *The Charlie Rose Show,*" November 15, 1999.

———, "Transcript: *The Late Show With David Letterman*," November 1999.

———, "Transcript: *The Tonight Show with Jay Leno*," June 27, 2003.

William Keck, "A Window into His Soul," *Los Angeles Times*, April 1, 2001. www.johnnydeppfan.com.

Christina Kelly, "Johnny Depp from A to W," *Sassy*, May 1990. www.johnnydeppfan.com.

Brendan Leman, "Johnny Depp," *Interview*, December 1995. www.johnnydeppfan.com.

Elizabeth McCracken, "Depp Charge," *Elle*, June 1998. www.johnny deppfan.com.

Holly Millea, "Ghost in the Machine," *Premiere*, February 1995. www.johnnydeppfan.com.

Cindy Pearlman, "Here's Johnny!" *Model*, December 1988. www.johnnydeppfan.com.

Jenny Peters, "Narcotics Synonymous," *GQ* (Australia), June 1998. www.johnnydeppfan.com.

Steve Pond, "Depp Perception," *US*, June 26, 1989. www.johnny deppfan.com.

Stephen Rebello, "Johnny Depp Lets Down His Hair," *Movieline*, April 1993. www.johnnydeppfan.com.

———, "Johnny Handsome," "*Movieline*, May 1990. www.johnny deppfan.com.

J. Sperling Reich, "Johnny Come Blow Your Horn," Reel.com. www.reel.com.

Tiffany Rose, "Hidden Deppths," *Cosmopolitan* (UK), June 2001. www.johnnydeppfan.com.

Rotten Tomatoes, "Johnny Depp." www.rottentomatoes.com.

James Ryan, "Depp Gets Deeper," *Vogue*, September 1994. www.johnnydeppfan.com.

Johanna Schneller, "Where's Johnny?" *Premiere*, December 1999. www.johnnydeppfan.com.

Kevin Sessums, "Johnny Be Good," *Vanity Fair*, February 1997. www.johnnydeppfan.com.

Dana Shapiro, "What Makes Johnny Famous?" *Icon*, June 1998. www.johnnydeppfan.com.

Tom Shone, "Johnny Depp Isn't Johnny Depp Anymore," *Talk*, October 1999. www.johnnydeppfan.com.

Tiscali Entertainment, "Depp Deals Hollywood a Blow." www. tiscali.co.uk.

VH1.com, "Biography: Iggy Pop." www.vh1.com.

Elaine Warren, "Bad Boy to Role Model," *TV Guide*, January 23, 1988. www.johnnydeppfan.com.

John Waters, "Johnny Depp," *Interview*, April 1990. www.johnny deppfan.com.

Clare Whipps, "Johnny Depp Talks Blow," Johnny Depp the Unofficial Site. www.johnyd3pp.20m.com.

Index

Picture Credits

About the Author

Kara Higgins lives in Piscataway, New Jersey, with her fiancé, George. She is currently the associate editor of *Twist* magazine, and she has done freelance work for magazines such as *YM*, *Cosmopolitan*, *Marie Claire*, and *New Jersey Monthly*. Raised in Marlton, New Jersey, she attended Cherokee High School and graduated from Rutgers University with a dual degree in journalism and communications. She loves writing, skiing, and visiting the Jersey Shore.